ZODIAC

LINCOLNSHIRE

Edited by Steve Twelvetree

First published in Great Britain in 2002 by
YOUNG WRITERS
Remus House,
Coltsfoot Drive,
Peterborough, PE2 9JX
Telephone (01733) 890066

HB ISBN 0 75433 578 X
SB ISBN 0 75433 579 8

FOREWORD

Young Writers was established in 1991 with the aim of promoting creative writing in children, to make reading and writing poetry fun.

Once again, this year proved to be a tremendous success with over 41,000 entries received nationwide.

The Zodiac competition has shown us the high standard of work and effort that children are capable of today. The competition has given us a vivid insight into the thoughts and experiences of today's younger generation. It is a reflection of the enthusiasm and creativity that teachers have injected into their pupils, and it shines clearly within this anthology.

The task of selecting poems was a difficult one, but nevertheless, an enjoyable experience. We hope you are as pleased with the final selection in *Zodiac Lincolnshire* as we are.

CONTENTS

Alice Pullinger	80
Olivia Musson	81
Joëlle Garland	82
Amy Sparks	83
Sophie Adams	84
Katherine Willoughby	84
Sophie Elgar	85
Fiona McLaughlin	86
Grace Costello	87
Danielle Winters	88
Heidi Maclachlan	89
Sarah Toulson	90
Charlotte Cleveland	91
Michelle Lee	92

Middlecott School

Nathan Cock	93
Kathryn Brewster	93
Linzee Vickers	94
Zoe Whitworth	94
Joe Roberts	95
Jonathan Storey	96
Charlene Blakey	96
Vicki Taylforth	97
Rory Young	97

Queen Elizabeth's High School

Katy Lamb	98
Hannah Norton	98
Drew Bowness	99
Angela Chan	100
Steve Robinson	100
Katie Shepherd	101
Claire Stringer	102
Stewart Simpkins	102
Vicky McIlroy	103
Harriet Tully	103
Alex Lee	104

The Poems

THE BATTLE OF THE MANY SEASONS

Jack and Orion were standing there in the middle
of the frosty battlefield
Then out of poppy heads shot Orion's troops
with a leaf and a root to wield
Then Jack Frost did make a storm and out of it
the enemy formed
Then suddenly started the fight which did commence
all through the night
But Jack Frost's attacks did fail and Orion's troops prevailed
Then Orion's saffron seeds did shoot and melted the enemy
into leaves and root
And that's how spring comes ever year and how Jack Frost
runs in fear waiting for revenge another year.

Andrew Burrell (12)
Ashvilla School

THE RIVETING FROG

This slimy fiend jumps from pond to pond.
Keeping its olive-coloured body well hidden.
Its webbed feet giving it an advantage to escape from danger.
Ducking and diving under hedgerows, creeping about in
deep vegetation.
Leaping from lily to lily, taking a rest every few leaps.
This creature lives a quiet, undercover life.
Keeping hidden from the outside world.
Rejected from a world of beautiful animals.
It sits back and relaxes, baking in the sun, keeping cool in the frosty,
but clear pond water.

Adam Cartwright (12)
Boston Grammar School

THE GOBLIN

This slimy, grey goblin
Hides away from life
He's always hidden in somethin'
Accompanied by his wife.

He has curled knife-sharp claws
And two beady eyes
Equipped with teeth like saws
And brick-solid thighs.

He likes it dark
Dark, damp and dreary not ablaze
To him it's a lark
His favourite place is under a dais.

For tea he appetisers in
Squid, worms and dried rye
And don't forget the gin
And for dessert he scoffs human pie.

In his time of leisure
Foot-head and naked tennis
Bring him much pleasure
But mostly he's just a menace.

This slimy, grey goblin
Hides away from life
He's always hidden in somethin'
Accompanied by his wife.

This tale is now told
And you may think it's nothin'
This is a promise that must be held
Stay away from the goblin!

Ben Carr (12)
Boston Grammar School

STARLIGHT

Stars are great
they shine really bright
they twinkle and shoot
but only at night

Some shoot across the sky
like a bullet from a gun
and some hang low
like they are just having fun

They are beautiful
amazing and bright
I stare at them in wonder
as they light up the night

They glisten and gleam
with strong beams of light
they light up my house
with their bright starlight

There are millions and millions
and maybe more
they cluster together
like dust on the floor

Stars are great
they shine really bright
they twinkle and shoot
but only at night.

Alex Faunt (12)
Boston Grammar School

Go, Go Gorilla

Go, go gorilla
The fastest gorilla around
Speedy here, speedy there
Speedy on the ground.

He whizzes through the jungle
At a lightning speed rate
He's always home for dinner
At around half past eight.

His long hairs wave
As he rages at his mighty pace
Practises all year round
To win the jungle race.

He lines up on the starting
Ready to unleash his speed
Bang! He's off
He moves like a growing weed.

Finished first
His task he has completed
He holds his medal in the air
He won the race fair and square

Go, go gorilla
The fastest gorilla around
Speedy here, speedy there
Speedy on the ground.

Thomas Brennan (13)
Boston Grammar School

DAWN 'TIL DUSK

We're in for another demanding day,
As the fruitless stubble awaits the plough.
Dolly and Jock, the dependable strength,
Await the master to mount their collars.
Collars fixed, they depart the stable,
Plough attached they leave the yard,
The farmer guides, as to the field they go.

Once in the field they bow their heads,
As they use their power to toil,
The farmer encourages from behind as the furrows turn,
A steady change from gold to brown unfolds.
Hunger calling, they take their break,
Sustenance supplied by the farmer's wife.
Back to work they've had their fill,
The field still needs completing,
Their heads now droop,
Awaiting their works fulfilment,
The warm autumn day begins to fade,
As the day draws to a close,
Dusk draws near, the pace slows down,
The farmer decides a day's work is done.

The plough unhitched, it's homeward-bound,
Once back in their stable it's time to rest,
Farmer welcomed by his devoted wife,
A bath to ease the aches and pains before slumber calls,
We're now ready for another day.

Daniel Welbourn (13)
Boston Grammar School

AUTUMN TIMES

The autumn comes swiftly in
with crispy, golden, brown leaves
they flap helplessly to the ground
gentle gusts scatter them for miles around
the crisp leaves flutter without any fight into a fire
from the human's Guy Fawkes night.

The sparklers glow, but soon go out and retire
the fireworks burst into light
making humans gasp and yell
the Catherine wheels spin wildly round
giving off a smoky smell.

Some creatures like hedgehog and co
try to sleep all the way through.

At Hallowe'en, children young and old
go off trick or treating
with monster masks
colours bold.

Soon it's Christmas time
presents many
some come cheap, some come dear
after that it's off into a different time
Here comes another new year!

Jack Hornsby (12)
Boston Grammar School

AUTUMN COMPLAINS

The chilly start to the day
The jewelled grass
And the foggy shrouds
All part of autumn's morn

As the leaves fall
The days get shorter
But the nights get longer
As animals prepare to hibernate

As I rustle through the crispy leaves
I listen to the wind howling
As the trees stand thin and bare
For autumn is in full force

Bonfire night is upon us
Bang! Whoosh! Pop!
As the fireworks scream upwards
People huddle around a bonfire

Autumn's here once again
For summer's fun will search in vain
There will no longer be any sun
Instead the autumn brings no fun.

Mark Bridges (12)
Boston Grammar School

STARS

Stars are beautiful,
Stars are bright.
They are absent by day
And twinkle at night.

Stars are fabulous,
Stars brightly shine.
I want to own them,
I wish they were mine.

Stars can shoot,
Stars can twinkle.
They get put on fir trees,
Surrounded by tinsel.

Stars are my favourite,
Stars are fine.
I really want one,
They're really divine.

Stars are beautiful,
Stars are bright.
They're absent by day
And twinkle all night.

James May (13)
Boston Grammar School

THE AUTUMN

September is the month in which autumn begins
The cold, the wind and the rain
Isn't it a pain
When you're stuck in the rain.

Howling winds blowing leaves off trees
Leaves all the branches bare
Children having fun
Collecting conkers in the cold.

Shorter days and longer nights
Isn't it a sign
A sign to say summer is over
What a shame.

Animals all in a hurry
Getting ready for winter
Birds flying south, others hibernating
They will return with the sun.

Now with the trees all bare
It's getting time to prepare
For a long, cold winter ahead
I think I'll just go to bed.

Adam Metssitane (12)
Boston Grammar School

SUBWAY SPIDER

S ubway spider
U nusually black as midnight
B eautiful in its own way
W ith seven dark yellow spots on the creature's back
A home under railway tracks, every night wide awake
Y ou see it curl up like a peanut, as a roaring train speeds past.

S ubway spider
P assionate about its life
I t ignores the giants screaming and trying to dismantle its body
D rowned in the waves of giants
E ventually it swims through
R age in its mind, but at least it has survived.

Johan Pickett (13)
Boston Grammar School

THE ZODIAC - AQUARIUS

A quarians are honest and loyal
Q uiet and peaceful
U nderstanding
A quarians love everyone between January 21st to February 18th
R ides the love of others
I n his heart he knows everyone within his reach
U nder his skin he has a heart of gold
S ucks up water and love, like you suck up fizzy drinks.

Jamie Bristow (12)
De Aston School

ZODIAC POEM

Each year is full of birthday signs,
To which we would agree,
Our dreams and wishes are often true,
Especially for me.

The moon and stars are there to shine,
Upon the people which are fine,
They sneak a look at secret times,
To judge themselves to different kinds.

Your dreams are caught in spider webs,
When we're tucked up warm in bed,
Your thoughts are mingled with ideas,
Then the moon and stars appear.

The fairies are light and quick,
And dart about very slick,
Feeding thoughts and making right,
All the outcomes of the night.

Josina Clarke (12)
De Aston School

LIBRA

The scales are my star sign
I am charming and urbane

On clear winter nights
Comets take their flight
Whizzing through the constellations . . .
Shining brightly as they go

You'll find me in the northern hemisphere
During the autumnal equinox.

Emily Howard (13)
De Aston School

MY LOVE

On the 23rd February,
We met unexpectedly,
It was love at first sight,
Luck was on my side . . .
At last.

You came into my life,
At a time you were needed most,
My life seemed worthless,
I wanted death at my door . . .
He never came.

But you came for me,
You made everything alright,
It finally made sense,
You and I were made . . .
For each other.

My love for you,
Is so strong and meaningful,
Never have I felt this way,
I'm so glad you came . . .
I mean that.

I have been so horrible,
I've hurt you at times,
Those days I really hated myself,
I didn't think I deserved you . . .
But you stood by me.

Why you still love me,
I really don't know,
The things that you say to me,
Make me feel special . . .
Thank you, my love.

Gemma Hayward (15)
De Aston School

WHAT ARE YOU?

When I lay in the sun,
When the day has just begun,
I wonder why I cannot fly,
Just like a bird in the morning sky.
What is your birthday date?
Can I be your new best mate?
Well, what are you?
If I am Scorpion!
What are you?
Are you a
Loving Libran?
Are you a
Sexy Sagittarian?
Are you a
Careful Capricorn?
Are you an
Amazing Aquarian?
Are you a
Pretty Piscean?
Are you an
Angry Aries?
Are you a
Tasty Taurus?
Are you a
Gorgeous Gemini?
Are you a
Cautious Cancerian?
Are you a
Laughing Leo?
Or are you a
Vivacious Virgo?

Siobhan Valerie Cunningham (12)
De Aston School

I'M NOT A FOOL!

I've got riters block
Mind you I can't rite.

I live down the dock
'You dont need to rite'
Me dad ses
So long as you can figh!

Hes quite happy for me to watch tv
But I wont beter than that.

They say Im stupid
Say Im thik
But that isnt' the truth.

Im just Dyslexic!

No one ever tried to help me
Makes me sic.
Even Instine was Dyslexic
He wosnt thik!

Just give me a chance
Ill be the next Newton.

I ate these competishions
Make me look like a fool.

What help have I got from school?
'Put her in bottom set, she's a fool!'

Ive got a new techer, who nows whats rong
Take time out to help

Says she nows what its like to struggle
Her bein black and al.

Thats al I need - a litle help
Ill be one working on Wall Street!

If its not too late . . .

Kate Hough (15)
De Aston School

CONTEMPLATE

The smooth handle in my grip,
whisper of the blade,
dragged from its sheath.

Contemplate the cold shine,
soon its place shall be mine.

Draw the blade from left to right,
embedded deep,
welcome the bite.

Pink flesh splits,
comes apart.

Red flows up to greet me,
splashes upon my face,
liquid warmth in the cool night.

Contemplate the cold shine,
now its peace is mine.

Colour dims,
lie on the floor,
close my eyes.

Anjuli Marwood-Afferby (15)
De Aston School

ZODIAC

Capricorn, ends and starts the yearly span,
Practical, patient, takes time to plan.

Aries, fun loving and confident,
Any money is quickly spent.

Gemini, the youthful and witty sign,
They talk a persuasive line.

Zodiac, from Pisces to Virgo,
Give all of us something to follow.

Laura Underwood (12)
De Aston School

SAGITTARIUS

S   trong
A   gile
G   regarious
I   ntelligent
T   ruculent
T   rustworthy
A   ctive
R   esponsible
I   nspiring
U   seful
S   porty.

Tiffany Bruntlett (12)
De Aston School

FIRST DAY AT KGGS

My eyes snap open,
What is it about today?
And then . . . I remember,
Today is the day I start my secondary school!

My heart thumps against my chest,
I am a drum being viciously beaten by my cruel oppressor.

My hands automatically knot my tie,
I am a stowaway inside someone else's brain.
I'm not really here,
Please tell me, I'm not here!

My mum drops me off outside the door,
I am shivery, freezing as ice.
I try to smile to my friends,
I am fine, I am not nervous, I am a liar.

I walk to the first lesson,
I am inhabited by a colony of flighty butterflies.
I sit down in the seat allocated for me,
I am a dream, wake up! Wake up!

It is lunch break, I walk around with a sixth former,
I am a rose; I am wilting with hunger.
I am shown all the rooms,
I am a sieve; information drops through me.
I go back to my form room,
I am a robot; I have no soul.

I am in my last lesson,
I am a person. Let me live in my dream.
A happy school. I am in a happy school.
I am in secondary school.
I am happy.

Victoria Rigby (11)
Kesteven & Grantham Girls' School

MY FIRST DAY AT SCHOOL

As I met the bottom of the stairs my heart sank,
As I knew I had to climb four flights
And would I have enough stamina?
I started to climb, it felt fine after one flight
But when I started the second flight
My legs hurt so badly.
I stopped to gaze out of the window,
When I spotted old friends from primary school.
I then got into my *form room.*
A form room, what is a form room?
Maybe it is a room where you fill out forms!
After all the information that was stuffed in our heads
And all the books covering the whole of our tables,
It was lunch, my favourite part of the day.
There was a variety to choose from.
Next was a 'treasure hunt' to help us find our way around school,
Since it was so big.
My partner and I came back to the start after forty-two minutes,
we had *finished.*
It was the end of school, we called it home time at primary school.
'See you tomorrow,' I said to all my friends.

Alison Huddart (11)
Kesteven & Grantham Girls' School

MY IDEAL FRIEND

Stay in and play, go out and play,
she doesn't mind.
It doesn't really matter to her,
as long as we have a good time!

Be excited, be happy,
you can be in a huff!
Whatever she does is always enough.

No secrets, no whispers,
we're always straight with each other.
No squabbles, no arguments,
we don't see why we should bother!

Stay truthful, stay honest,
that's the way you should be.
Well actually, there's really no need!

Grace Alexander (11)
Kesteven & Grantham Girls' School

GONE AWAY

When I've gone away,
Remember me,
Gone away to a far away land,
When I can no longer hold your little hand,
Nor can I be here and stay,
Gone away day by day,
Nor can we do what you had planned,
I'm going away you must understand,
All I can ask is for you to pray,
To know I can no longer stay,
Afterwards do not grieve and grieve,
The love between us will never leave,
It will be better for you if you can be happy,
And me to be sad, sad to leave you,
Always remember to smile,
And in your heart I shall be no longer than a mile,
So I'll be back,
Back here with you,
Now don't cry,
Bye my little doll, bye.

Emma Lynch (11)
Kesteven & Grantham Girls' School

FIRST DAY AT KGGS

The giant school stands before me,
It's the scariest day of my life,
My tie is close to strangling me,
And my thoughts are as sharp as a knife.

Girls are blue as crayons,
Girls as blue as the sea,
Teachers are hustling and rushing,
And thank heavens not looking at me.

The bell rings for the start of school,
The footsteps are like earthquakes,
And then the slamming of lockers,
As my body starts to shake.

Lunch is in the canteen,
With queues as long as could be,
But everything was okay,
Because I have packed today.

At the end of school,
I am a KG girl,
Walking down the road,
With my heavy load.

Elizabeth Anthony (11)
Kesteven & Grantham Girls' School

THE OWL

He sits there and waits
Until it becomes dark
He will then turn around and look at the ground
Along comes a tiny mouse, unaware of his adventure ahead
He will then swoop down, as quick as a flash.

The claws get hold of the poor, little mouse
Who squeaks madly trying to break free
He then flies back and adds the mouse to his stack
About an hour later he's found some more
His meal is complete, now it's time for a snack.

Kerry Nix (12)
Kesteven & Grantham Girls' School

LISTEN TO THE DOLPHINS CALLING

Watching the sunrise setting on the sparkling ocean
Tall ships gliding through the gentle breeze
Listen to the dolphins calling
Trees blowing in the gentle breeze
Autumn is on its way
Listen to the dolphins calling
Leaves falling off the trees
Leaves blowing towards you and around your feet
Listen to the dolphins calling
Dressing up in woolly jumpers and warm clothing
Snuggling up to a fire on a cold night to get warm
Listen to the dolphins calling
Toes, fingers going all numb
From the coldness outside and the warmth in
Listen to the dolphins calling
Squirrels darting back and forth
Gathering nuts and berries ready for the cold winter
Listen to the dolphins calling
Jack Frost knocks on your window every morning
Waking up to a white and foggy view
Listen to the dolphins calling.

Chelsea Smith (11)
Kesteven & Grantham Girls' School

AUTUMN

The autumn leaves, they drift
The autumn leaves, they swoop
Making a quilt of warmth on the ground

The trees, they are bare
The trees, they are left cold
They are longing for spring to come and wrap up warm

The plants, they die
The plants, they shiver
They are covered by the wonderful falling leaves

The children, they play
The children, they are wrapped up warm
They toss leaves into the air, letting them fall like rain

The weather, it changes
The weather, it becomes evil
It blows, making people stay in their fire lit homes

The birds, they fly gracefully
The birds, they escape coldness
They set off for warmer climates

The animals, they become cold
The animals, they suffer
They find hiding places to hide in until spring

The colours, they change
The colours, they are beautiful
Red, orange, yellow, bronze and gold.

Laura Beckett (12)
Kesteven & Grantham Girls' School

PARADISE

The sun, the sea, the sand,
This is paradise.
Swimming with dolphins,
This is paradise.
The ocean is lapping,
This is paradise.
Listening to the waterfalls falling,
This is paradise.
Walking through the rainforest,
This is paradise.
The sound of the birds,
This is paradise.
Looking at the tropical animals,
This is paradise.
Streams are trickling,
This is paradise.
Shaded by palm trees,
This is paradise.
The calling of whales,
This is paradise.
The thought of being alone on a desert island,
This is paradise.
Watching the fish swimming gracefully underwater,
This is paradise.
Sleeping in a hammock,
This is paradise.
Paradise is this.

Rachel Turpie (11)
Kesteven & Grantham Girls' School

THE PICTURE

A stranger called this morning
Dressed all in black and grey
Put every colour in a bag
And carried them away

The tongue, tickling red of the strawberry ice lolly
The fiery, fun yellow of the sun bright and jolly
The sparkling, soft blue of the sea wide and deep
The glistening, sharp pink of the sweets for me to keep
The pastel, smudged orange of the beautiful sunset
The startling, quick gold of the shooting comet

Who is this man that's taken all the colours away?
I know the mouth, I know that nose
He's asking people to sit and pose
For a *charcoal portrait!*

Siobhan Croft (11)
Kesteven & Grantham Girls' School

KATHRYN

Kind and loyal
Friendly and clever
We will stay friends
Forever and ever

Fun to be with
Lively and bright
We get on so well
We scarcely fight

We like the same things - it's great!
She really is my best mate!

Agnes C Jacobs (11)
Kesteven & Grantham Girls' School

SPRINGTIME

Hibernation is over
Animals come out
Crunch, crunch
Animals walking over leaves and twigs
It starts to get warmer and warmer
Nuts and berries all over the ground
The forest starts talking again with chitty-chatter
Buds bursting through the ground
Pink flowers start to appear on the trees
Birds lay their eggs
All the animals get ready to have offspring
Making sure their homes are nice and comfy for the arrival
of their young
Their babies finally arrive
Lots of learning to be done
Waiting for their eyes to open
Mums find food for their babies
Colour comes back to the forest
When their eyes open they see the world for the first time
Their first steps, or their first flight
Very special, very important
Slowly they learn to walk or fly
Watch out, bump!
Oh dear, they keep falling over
When they fly or when they walk
That is the end of springtime!

Abigail Underwood (11)
Kesteven & Grantham Girls' School

HELP!

Help I'm being bullied
Somebody help me
I'm scared
I wish they would just leave me alone
I didn't do anything
It's painful
It hurts
If nobody helps me I'll scream
I mean it
Help me
Somebody
Please
I'm trapped, there's no way out
Stuck in a nightmare
Help
Wake me up
I just want this to stop
Otherwise my life is
Over
They will stop
They got me
My
Life
Is
Over
Help!

Kirstie Philpot (11)
Kesteven & Grantham Girls' School

DOGGING AROUND!

Finger chewing
Neck licking
Biscuit crunching
Fast running
Human loving
Book ripping
Twig snapping
Cat scaring
Ear pricking
TV watching
Ball catching
Food sniffing
Rabbit chasing
Tail wagging
Flea scratching
Sausage stealing
Water slurping
Postman biting
Ankle nipping
River swimming
Bone burying
Hole digging
Teeth baring
Puddle making
Man's best friend
The dog!

Leanne Murphy (11)
Kesteven & Grantham Girls' School

LIGHT

As the sun gets lower in the sky,
The moon rises like a watching eye,
Higher it gets as the night draws near,
It's a wonderful time so what do some people fear?

The stars appear one by one,
I look up and see the sun has now gone.

Lighting up the sky like a big glitter ball,
The moon is shining the brightest of them all.
The sky has changed colour from blue to black,
The morning will soon come and the sun will be back.

When you watch carefully you can see the change
Of day to night,
Dawn comes with the sun and brings back the light.

Kathryn Hodgson (11)
Kesteven & Grantham Girls' School

TRUE FRIENDS

You're with him and not with me,
Your only true friend for eternity.
You make me laugh,
He makes me cry,
Please don't let me say goodbye.

I'll always be here till the end of time,
Listening to you whinge and whine.
You may be mad,
You may be bad,
Please don't forget me, it will make me sad.

You've always been there when I've needed you,
And visa versa,
I've been there for you too,
I'll never forget the things we've done,
You'll find out who true friends are in time to come.

Aimee Bidwell (12)
Kesteven & Grantham Girls' School

UNTITLED

Silver-grey, flitting in the moonlight,
Leaving soft tracks on the hard snow.
Crying for family, crying for food,
Tempted by the bait in the traps,
On the bloodstained leaves.

Sweeping as a shadow
And gliding as a breeze,
Tab, tab, tab,
Creeping silently as death,
A ghost of moonlight.

Yellow eyes burning in the darkness,
Burning as twin flames,
The rustle of leaves, the snap of a twig,
The shining moonlight reflecting on a frightened, dewy eye,
All would be welcome.
None came.

Like a wisp from a cobweb,
Sliding in the shadows,
Creeping away from the sneaking dawn,
All alone, dying.
A wolf.

Gina Borriello (12)
Kesteven & Grantham Girls' School

THE WATER

The cool, calm water laps over the rocks,
the wind blows through the tall palm trees.
The beautiful sun sparkles on the small opening ripples,
the water trickles over the grey mixed with blue stones and shells.
The surface of the waters opening is filled with fish
and bubbles surface in the water like champagne in a glass.
The seagulls watch anxiously waiting, knowing if they're going to get
a catch,
the white clouds drift across the sky like floating balls of cotton wool.

The day soon turns to night and becomes dark
and the sun rests up on the horizon.
The moon takes over the dark night,
and the warm feeling of the sun soon turns cold.
The moonlight shines over the dark blue, cold sea
and everything is very quiet, apart from the consecutive noise from
the sea.

Daniella Squires (11)
Kesteven & Grantham Girls' School

STARS

Stars are beautiful, stars are bright
Forever twinkling through the dark night
When they sit there in the sky
I wonder why they are so very high

Zodiacs are to do with stars
Pisces, Capricorn and Leos
If I was Chinese I would be a horse
If you're a Leo or a horse
You are best, of course

Stars talk to each other, they go clubbing at night
That's why they glow with such pure white light
Stars are beautiful, stars are bright
Forever twinkling through the night.

Eleanor Jane Rusk (11)
Kesteven & Grantham Girls' School

SWEET 16!

Recently I turned 16!
16 . . . sweet 16,
Now, what's so special about being 16?
It's funny . . .
Seems like yesterday I turned 6!
And last week I was a baby.
I'm not a baby anymore . . .
No. I'm a woman! Grown-up! Teenager.
So, if 16 is so special . . .
What's new?
I'm not any taller, smarter or thinner . . .
And definitely not a year wiser!
To be honest . . . the older I get the more mistakes I make!
After all, I'm a teenager . . .
And me being a teenager would like to cause trouble,
mayhem and torment!
So hear me *roar!*
Hear the cry of a teenager! Woman!
Grown-up!
And you'll realise that 16 . . .
Well . . .
Isn't so special!
So sweet . . .

Hannah Y Y Chan (16)
Kesteven & Grantham Girls' School

MY FIRST DAY AT SECONDARY SCHOOL

It was here at last,
Nerves had taken over me,
I was like a frightened mouse.

Questions buzzing round my head,
Soon find out it isn't so bad,
I was like a newborn lamb.

My mum waved goodbye,
I walk into the Robert's Hall,
I was as excited as a bunny springing around.

It's lunchtime now, this is new,
I choose a jacket potato with beans,
I felt as happy as a child at Christmas.

We are having a treasure hunt now,
Whizzing through the questions, this is fun,
I was dashing around like a colony of ants.

It's time to go home,
It's been a long day,
I felt as proud as a peacock.

Sarah Cruickshank (11)
Kesteven & Grantham Girls' School

MY FIRST DAY AT SCHOOL

Waiting
Waiting for my bus to come
Screech!
We all cram on
Another screech came and I was finally at KGGS

I felt scared and really nervous
I went down a little further and plunged to a stop
At the top of what I call a mountain

I ventured up four flights of stairs
I finally reached the top
Opened my class door and sat in my chair.

'Ding ding!' the bell went to leave school
I was walking out of the school
Like a slow tortoise not knowing his way home
Home
My favourite place.

Lindsay Ash (11)
Kesteven & Grantham Girls' School

WHY DO I HAVE TO BE DIFFERENT?

Eyes look right through me with cold-hearted stares,
I'm just sitting, waiting for someone to call me names.
Waiting . . . to be picked last in PE,
Oh, why do I have to be different?

I want to have friends, to fit in,
Am I really so bad,
So disgusting that no one will come near me?
Please Lord, tell me why I have to be different?

I wish the teacher would know it's OK to hug me when I score,
And that it hurts inside when people point fun.
I really love where I live and I don't want to leave,
But maybe I have no choice . . .

Now when I fall they help me up,
When I am sad they make me feel so much better,
When I laugh they laugh with me, not at me,
And when I'm scared they help me through.
Thank you everyone for now I am not different!

Emma Brown (11)
Kesteven & Grantham Girls' School

MY FIRST DAY AT KGGS

My first day at my new school,
I looked as neat as a pin.
My new rucksack on my back,
Anxious for the day to begin.

I strolled with anticipation,
Into the Robert's Hall.
Equipment seemed much bigger here,
I began to feel quite small.

Faces full of expression,
As children and teachers meet.
Nervous apprehension,
As friends for life I greet.

The lunchtime bell seemed early,
And I queued with all the rest.
For delights of the cafeteria,
I prepared to try and test.

The afternoon passed swiftly,
As new subjects came abound.
Netball, French and Latin,
Interests all around.

A first day's hard work over,
And I get back on the bus.
I'm feeling so excited,
I can't help but make a fuss.

Sophie Carter (11)
Kesteven & Grantham Girls' School

AUTUMN

Autumn is when
The wind blows the trees
Autumn is when
The trees lose their leaves

Autumn is when
The leaves are about
Autumn is when
The sweepers come out

Autumn is when
The nights draw in
Autumn is when
The conker fights begin

Autumn is when
The leaves become gold
Autumn is when
The weather gets cold

Autumn is when
The farmers harvest
Autumn is when
The fruit and corn is ripest

Autumn is when
The wind blows the trees
Autumn is when
The trees lose their leaves.

Amy Britton (12)
Kesteven & Grantham Girls' School

MOONLIGHT SHADOWS

Lost, I walk into the walls of blackness,
Scared, no sound just the darkness sucking me into its land of sadness,
Shivering, the unhappiness surrounds me, leaving no escape.

Then the moon gleaming, trying to show me the way out,
It's doing very well sparkling in the sky,
But dark fights back blowing out the light like a candle.

Now I am scared again, no one to help, the moon failed,
I'm alone again, or am I?
Sounds start to build - insects, owls and sounds I've never heard before.

I look round searching for a way out,
But nothing, I'm surrounded by shadows,
Something moved, my heart beating rapidly,
The moon is back, the shadows are dancing trying to catch me,
I run and follow the moonlight.

Susan Newbould (11)
Kesteven & Grantham Girls' School

FIRST DAY AT SCHOOL

A day in a strange new place,
Children rushing back and forth,
Running from place to place.
I heard someone say, 'Who's she?'
I want to go home!

A brand new school
The most boring place on Earth!
But wait, one problem, not more homework!
Hold on what was that teacher's name again?
Where do I go next?
Where is that room?
I want to go home!

When's lunch?
I'm starving!
When's the bell going to go?
I want freedom!
I want to go to bed!
I want to go home!

Holly Brook (12)
Kesteven & Grantham Girls' School

A Baby Is A ...

A baby is a . . .

Loud crying
Book ripping
Dummy sucking
Nappy wetting
Milk drinking
Stroppy padding
Hair pulling
Messy eating
Lolly sucking
Party wrecking
Mummy kissing
Game spoiling
Sister hating
Sweetie munching
Chocolate loving
Nose picking
Toy pinching
Loud screaming
Cheeky laughing

Pest!

Leanne Lewin (11)
Kesteven & Grantham Girls' School

Summer, Winter And Spring

You will find in my garden every sort of green
I think summers are the best
They're sunny and they're warm
And every time the sun comes out
I'm really happy with glee.

I really like the swing
That hangs above my head from the strongest branch
From my lovely big, green tree
And the snow comes down in winter
It makes me think about the sun
And the happiness it brings to lovely little me.

But in spring when the flowers grow
And little creatures crawl out of the hedgerow
I'm really, really happy
'Cause it means that summer will be up n the leaves
Of my lovely big, green tree.

But I still think that Saturdays in summer are the best
Because I live beside the sea
And when we walk our dog over the hills
I can see the big blue sea!
And every night when I swing on my swing
I really can't wait till spring.

Nicola Bathard (11)
Kesteven & Grantham Girls' School

The Sea

Tidal waves reaching high in the sky,
Storms reaching gale force 9.
Large whirlwinds shattering ships,
Ships sinking to the bottom of the ocean.

The strong currents washing away unknown territories,
Swarms of fish fighting the kings of the sea.
Surfers surfing, breaking through the foam,
Lighthouses blinking warning sailors to watch out for rocks.

Kimberley Charity (12)
Kesteven & Grantham Girls' School

FIRST DAYS AT SECONDARY SCHOOL

My first day of torture,
What is it going to be like?
I bet the homework's a real scorcher,
Have the teachers ever gone on strike?

I'm here, but it seems strange,
As I stagger up the stairs,
I know this is a big change,
And us girls are dying to wear flares!

I open the door,
I see all these faces,
And then I see more,
Where is my place?

Time to settle down,
I haven't made any friends yet,
The teacher gives me a frown,
Oh well, I'd better do the work that's set.

I listen for the bell,
3 . . . 2 . . . 1 . . .
Then suddenly I yell
'Today's been great fun!'

Poppy Duffree (11)
Kesteven & Grantham Girls' School

MY HOUSE

Up at the top
 Is a bathroom
  And three bedrooms
   A few steps down
    You will find a bookcase
     And if you are there in the night
      This piece of furniture may give you a fright
     Right at the bottom
      Are some pegs holding coats
     Also there is
      A front room and a kitchen
     And to complete the tour
    Go straight ahead
    And out the front door.

Charley Hranyczka (11)
Kesteven & Grantham Girls' School

FIRST DAY AT SCHOOL

At school I am just like a fish,
Lost in an ocean of bags, coats and hockey sticks
Drowning in a sea of books, forms and homework
We've only been here five minutes and already
I've lost my bus pass, again!
Everyone else knows where to go
How come it's only me gets lost?
I trudge up what feels like seventy flights of stairs
And when I finally lug myself up all those steps
I find myself in the wrong classroom
Miles away from where I am supposed to be
And I haven't even got past the first hour yet!

Natalie Hamilton (12)
Kesteven & Grantham Girls' School

SCHOOL?

The bus coughs to a stop as its eerie horn screeches
and I stumble out of bed
I swim through bags and coats to get to the back
Half asleep, I arrive
Gazing wearily up at its tall body
It's thinking, yum! Another victim to swallow up!
The window, its milky eye staring at me, wickedly.

Forever lasting corridors leading you to its trap
Standing below what seemed like a mountain to me
I venture up four flights of stairs
Wondering when they will end.

Trapped in a jungle of unfamiliar creatures
I follow its twisted body to the next room
Silence
I hear it breathing steadily
Lessons
What are lessons? One of its other plans to keep me in?
Homework
I never knew it existed.

Walking peacefully out of school
I wait patiently for the bus
Bus? Will it ever come?
Its milky eye watching my every move
Watching, waiting, watching, waiting . . .
Beep beep! Beep beep! My alarm clock, 8.30
Time for my first day of school.

Katie Hills (11)
Kesteven & Grantham Girls' School

WOODLAND STORIES

Up, up, up the sun is waking,
Filling the sky with warmth and love
Shining its beautiful rays upon the land,
Tree leaves rustle in the mild breeze.
The day progresses, the animals come out,
Rabbits and squirrels collect food
The sun smiles down upon them,
Tree leaves rustle in the mild breeze.
Midday draws closer,
The sun reaches its hottest peak
It's now too warm to play,
Tree leaves rustle in the mild breeze.
Dawn will soon be here,
The badgers will soon be out
The owl is stirring in his sleep,
Tree leaves rustle in the mild breeze.
The sun is tired, it's sinking into the horizon.
The animals run off to bed,
The badgers and owls come out to hunt
Tree leaves rustle in the mild breeze.

Ayesha Dunk (11)
Kesteven & Grantham Girls' School

THE HURRICANE

It pounds and punches along the beach,
Crashing and smashing, beating and bashing,
Slicing and slashing mercilessly.
Whipping and whirling, twisting and twirling,
The hurricane works its way out of the sea.

Swishing and swallowing, dipping and wallowing,
The hurricane works its way up to its foes.
Slipping and sliding, it keeps colliding,
Pulling a tree with it as it goes.

Alive and wild, it has a will,
A will of iron, it intends to live.
But the iron is melting, less strength every minute,
Trying to hide away from the heat.

Destroying the dust, it's dying, dying,
Every second and it's trying, trying.
The iron is melted, the hurricane lives no more.
But hurricane's havoc is left behind,
For others to organise again.

Annis Cordy (11)
Kesteven & Grantham Girls' School

WHAT AM I?

I have the head of an ape,
Big and very hairy.
The neck of a giraffe,
Extended and speckly.
The shoulders and arms of a fish,
Slimy and wet.
A torso of a lion,
Broad and proud.
A belly of supermodel,
Small and what do I eat?
The hips of a cat,
Furry and full of fleas.
The legs of a child,
Scarred and scabby.
The feet of an elephant,
Grey and wrinkly.
What am I again?
I really *don't know!*

Michaela Welsh (11)
Kesteven & Grantham Girls' School

FIRST DAY AT SCHOOL

A day at a brand new school
Being squashed in the corridors by children
I don't know which way to go
Lots of rooms forget which one
Unbelievably strange and terrifyingly large
I finally get to my rightful place

Four flights of stairs to climb
Lots of people you don't know (who are they?)
It's like small fish in an ocean
You get to your form room
Start talking to people
Great! I've met some friends

What will I do next?
Where will I go?
Phew! The teacher's coming
She writes the lessons on the board
Eight lessons to go till the end of the day
Oh no! It's going to be ages

The first lesson is at ten past nine
The last lesson is at five past three
Eight lessons which room are they in?
Follow everyone else
See which room they go in
Or are they lost as well?

When's lunchtime?
I hope it's soon, I'm hungry
Yes! The bell's just gone
Oh no! There's a long queue
I'm going to be standing here for ages
Glad when I get home.

Katie Howitt (11)
Kesteven & Grantham Girls' School

THE BATTLE OF THE SUNELVEN REALM

The day that dawned was bleak, grey and misty,
The air was charged with tension and hatred,
As two great armies gathered together:
The Sunelven army, in their red cloaks,
The Moonelven army, in their blue capes,
Each army bearing a streaming pennant,
Their horses snort and shift uneasily,
Adorned in glinting, silver finery,
Their manes and tails plaited and braided,
Suddenly, battle cries sliced through the air.

Horses reared, and they charged into battle,
Steel clashed on steel, and arrows flew,
Bloodcurdling battle cries rent the air,
The terrible battle raged back and forth,
For the power of the Sunelven Realm,
Till the Sunelven captain was cut down,
The heartened Moonelven army surged forth,
The brave Sunelven army stood their ground,
Their newly elected chief urged them on,
They regrouped and fought with a new technique.

The Sunelven army's new technique
Thwarted the Moonelven army, who fled,
Leaving the Moonelven captain behind,
The Sunelven army quickly seized him,
Demanding to know where his men had fled,
Threatened with death, he told them the right place,
The next day, they recruited and set off,
They took over the Moonelven castle,
Renamed it, and took them all prisoners,
Treating them fairly: the battle was won.

Georgina Grundy (11)
Kesteven & Grantham Girls' School

FRIENDS

Friends are always there for you
Even when you've got the flu
When you're feeling a little blue
Friends then tell you what to do!

We go shopping when it's sunny
And love to spend lots of money
The street entertainers are really funny
One does a trick and produces a bunny!

Saturday is disco night
With parent strictly out of sight
We love to see the laser light
The atmosphere is always just right

In the holidays we play
Tennis, cricket and games all day
We like to swim but have to pay
But it's free to bike along the way

So now I've told you what I do
With my friend
Oh, by the way, her name's Sue!

Amber Smith (11)
Kesteven & Grantham Girls' School

SEASONS

In springtime lambs are born,
Flowers start blooming,
Fields of daffodils brighten up the summer countryside.

Summer comes next and brightens up the sky,
Shorts and T-shirts, buckets and spades,
A holiday from school is my favourite bit.

Leaves change colour, must be autumn,
Conkers are falling from the trees,
Witches and vampires, must be Hallowe'en,
Trick or treating is in fashion these years.

Icy snow, winter is here,
Lights are put up, must be near to Christmas,
Presents and turkeys, snowmen and snow fights.

Jessica Bland (11)
Kesteven & Grantham Girls' School

DEEP BLUE OCEAN

The waves gently lap the seashore
The gentle ocean whispers softly
Deep blue crystal ocean
My wispy hair is caught by the gentle winds
The soft, silent winds whirl through my hair
Deep blue crystal ocean.

The beautiful ocean sunset fills my heart with joy
The magnificent colours look fantastic in the dark, dull sky
Deep blue crystal ocean
The sea has a silver layer of liquid
Across the top of the ocean
Deep blue crystal ocean.

My body is filled with gladness from the beautiful
whispers from the ocean
Deep blue crystal ocean
The morning comes and the ocean shimmers
From her sleep all is well and right
Deep blue crystal ocean.

Hollie Jackson (11)
Kesteven & Grantham Girls' School

THE TIGRESS

Black and orange against the long yellow grass,
The tigress of the Indian plain is not seen.
Oblivious, the gazelle is nearing her death.
One more move and the prey will be caught . . .
The Bengal tigress slowly approaches,
Laid back, muscles burning with tension.
Not a sound the tigress makes, until . . .
The gazelle pauses, and looks up.
What was that sound in the long grass?
Ears pricked forward, the gazelle is alert.

Listening for any sounds at all, worried for her life,
The gazelle snorts, she recognises that smell somehow . . .
Gathering energy in her hind legs, ready to spring away,
The prey finally senses the Bengal tigress' presence.
The camouflaged predator realises,
This is her last chance, she needs food . . . soon.
Snarling and growling, the tigress pounces,
She misses and so is led a wild dance for her meal.
A final leap from the gazelle sends her soaring,
Only to be killed instantly with one single slash of claw.

Gorging on the warm flesh, the tigress is fed,
She is content, she has drank her blood for the while.
Effortlessly she hides the rest of the carcass,
The meat will save for another day.
Her strong, handsome face is speckled with blood,
Roaring a challenge to all enemies.
She marks her territory on a nearby tree,
Then pads away into the distance.
The roar confirmed her power, her control,
Forever she would roam India.

Claire Reynolds (11)
Kesteven & Grantham Girls' School

SHE WALKS ...

Down the misty beach,
Walks the mysterious figure.
Dressed in old rags,
Long hair hiding her face.

Crashing waves hit the rocks,
She walks silently past,
As if on a mission,
She reaches the cliff edge.

She dives down, down, down,
Falling, falling, falling.
Crashing in treacherous waters,
Swimming into rolling waves.

Towards an isolated island,
She reaches the beach.
Glancing back at the coast,
With tears streaming down her face.

Running into the forest,
She did not return.
I stood and watched,
I waited and waited.

She did not come,
Suddenly a little seal appeared.
It slid into the water,
It bobbed around for a while.

I watched it with eager eyes,
It dived down into the depths.
I hoped it would return,
But I never saw the seal, or the girl again.

Sarah McClenaghan (11)
Kesteven & Grantham Girls' School

ROLLER COASTER

I've left my tummy way up there
It's given me quite a scare
Up and down
And all around
My screams black out any other sound
Tipping, turning
My tummy's squirming
Chugging up to the very top
Will this ride ever stop?
My family is standing way below
Mum and Dad are waving hello
It's so unfair, why won't they come?
It's always me who has the fun!
It's all so fast, it's just a blur
Is that Mum? I can't see her
I can't tell, I'm upside down
Is she smiling or is it a frown?
Finally we start to slow
My turn is over, it's time to go!

Georgie Hollands (11)
Kesteven & Grantham Girls' School

THE ROSE

Soaring up towards the sky,
Full of beauty and of charm,
Gives happiness to everyone,
A lonely scarlet rose.

The scent of its perfume,
The mixture of colours,
Petals so soft to touch,
A lonely scarlet rose.

When the actual rose is gone,
Its memory lives on,
It's always there in our hearts and our minds,
A lonely scarlet rose.

Alice Riches (13)
Kesteven & Grantham Girls' School

WHO ARE THEY?

They scream and shout,
They stamp their feet,
They push in queues,
They hate children
But work with them,
They're always in a bad mood!
They're demons,
They're vampires in disguise!
They give you too much homework,
They can't be human!
They must be robots!
You know when they're going to tell you off,
Their eyes narrow - almost closed,
They think they're so much better than we are,
They *never* admit when they're wrong!
They make you tidy what isn't your mess!
They're always saying,
'Tuck your shirt in,'
'Make sure your chair is under,'
And the dreaded,
'Your homework is . . .'
What are these *mad* things?
Answer: *Teachers!*

Lucy Sheehan (11)
Kesteven & Grantham Girls' School

AUTUMN

The hot summer's over,
The cool autumn's here,
The sun hides away for most of the day,
The fog is like a big blanket hiding things from view.

Frogs hide away under old logs,
Hedgehogs curl up so they look like a ball,
Then they sleep the winter away,
They finally wake up when the spring arrives,
Squirrels and mice gather together lots of food,
To prepare for a cold winter ahead,
Birds migrate from one country to another.

Leaves go crispy and brown on trees,
Then they finally flutter to the ground,
Leaving the tree like a skeleton in the wind,
Children play with the hard conkers,
Gathered from under the chestnut trees,
The crops are harvested and the fields are ploughed.

It gets colder every day,
Winter's on its way!

Laura Mottershead (11)
Kesteven & Grantham Girls' School

MY FIRST DAY AT SECONDARY SCHOOL

The evening before I couldn't sleep
How would I fit in?
The evening before and I was so excited
A new part of my life about to begin

The morning arrived and still apprehensive
I set off on my new journey
The butterflies in my stomach alive
A new part of my life about to begin

The school looked cold and grey
The fear growing inside me
In the hall were friendly faces
A new part of my life about to begin

New friends, new teachers, new rules
The butterflies flying away
The fear was gone, the adventure began
A new part of my life about to begin.

Sarah-Jane Harrison (12)
Kesteven & Grantham Girls' School

WHEN I . . .

When I hear the silence,
I feel peaceful.
When I see the underwater world,
I feel part of something special.
When I see the dolphins jumping,
I want to jump with them.
When I hear the dolphins calling,
I want to reply.

When I touch the silky sand,
I want to curl up in it.
When I feel the water rushing past me,
I feel powerful.
When I know I'm all alone,
I wonder why, I want to know.
When I catch a glimpse of shimmering sun,
I know that in sharing this unique place,
I would be sharing a special dream.
One world nobody knew existed.
My world.

Amy Johnson (13)
Kesteven & Grantham Girls' School

ME AND MY FRIENDS

Me and my friends have so much fun,
We play in the rain or in the sun.
We see each other every week,
And we sometimes play hide-and-seek!

Me and my friends stick together,
But sometimes one of us will lose our tether.
A lot of the time we're in town,
And we cheer each other up when we are down!

Me and my friends have known each other for ages,
During my life I could have written pages,
On the things that we used to get up to,
And I have lots of memories of the things we used to do!

Me and my friends have sleepovers,
But we named them don't sleepovers,
This is because we barely ever sleep,
And to get to sleep we have to count sheep!

My friends are one in a million
And nothing could ever replace them!

Jade Wainwright (11)
Kesteven & Grantham Girls' School

AUTUMN

September begins, the end of summer
Memories of long, hot days
The nights are drawing in
Autumn begins.

The leaves are falling from the trees
The wind gathers them up and they flicker on the breeze
Brilliant colours - yellow, brown, bronze, gold
What a brilliant sight to behold.

The animals gathering food for the winter
The squirrels gathering their nuts
It will soon be time to hibernate
Sleeping through the long, cold winter.

Yippee, Christmas is coming
The autumn colours make way for snow and frost
Frosty mornings are coming, get your slippers on
Put your hats and scarves on, on that special day.

Rebecca Underwood (11)
Kesteven & Grantham Girls' School

MY PETS

I've got nine pets altogether
A cat called Harriet
She's as light as a feather
Another cat called Tabitha
Tabby for short.
When she was a kitten
She used to get her collar caught.
A dog called Sadie
Who plays football
I wish I could play
But I always fall.
Five rabbits
Four girls and one boy
Who eat all the time
And play with lots of toys
And last but not least
A fish
Who is a golden colour
So I made a wish.

Amy Cook (11)
Kesteven & Grantham Girls' School

WRITING A POEM

'A poem,' she said, that teacher of mine,
'Is what you will write, in verse or in rhyme.'
No hint of a subject, no helpful ideas,
'Take care with your writing, no smudges or smears!'

I thought and I puzzled, I puzzled and thought,
So anxious to please and do what I ought,
But where should I start and where should I end?
The end should, I'm told, on the first verse depend.

And what of the rhyme,
Should it scan in waltz time?
With a one two three, one two three,
Found in each line?

I put pen to paper and started to write,
The time passed quite quickly and into the night,
And when at daybreak, I paused to reflect,
My good night's sleep I had found to neglect.

So here is my poem for better or worse,
With oh, so much thought put into each verse,
I hope she will like it, give ten out of ten,
But I expect she will say 'Go do it again!'

Emily Riley (12)
Kesteven & Grantham Girls' School

HOW DECEIVING THE DARK CAN BE

I see the raindrops falling down,
See the sunshine through the clouds,
See the colours of the town,
See the rushing of the crowds,
See this from my vantage point up high,
See the stars in the sky,

See the fields of wheat and rye,
See the birds as they fly by,
See it all spread out, beneath my feet,
My eyes look down and with them meet,
A vacant space, full of nothing,
A blanket of dark.

Elizabeth Kerr (13)
Kesteven & Grantham Girls' School

BELFAST CONFLICT

Boom!
A bomb explodes on the street outside
Scattering debris near and far
The smell of the explosion in everyone's nostrils
The sound of ringing in their ears.

'Extra!
Fourteen dead in last bombing'
Newspapers shout from every stand
While the world around sleeps in fear
Fear of being the next target.

Tap, tap!
The noise of soldiers' footsteps
Parading up and down the streets
Many peer out from behind lacy curtains
Then shrivel back in fear.

Shh!
Listen, do you hear it?
The faint sound of crying
It is that of humanity
Slowly dying, gradually each day.

Harriet Earle (13)
Kesteven & Grantham Girls' School

WHO LIKES SCHOOL DINNERS ANYWAY?

Plastic pizza squirming its way through the tray,
Toad in the hole which is missing its croaking toad,
Rubbery sausages which ping when you cut them,
Who likes school dinners anyway?

Jade mushy peas turning crusty on top,
Watery orange carrots which seem to wiggle their way down,
Sticky sweetcorn underneath piles of sloppy gravy,
Who likes school dinners anyway?

Are there really maggots in the mash?
The creamed potato surely isn't cold ice cream,
The jackets cement your insides, like trying to eat tar,
Who likes school dinners anyway?

Custard with lumps the size of snowballs,
Repulsive fruit we dare each other to eat,
Crimson jam doughnuts which clamp your teeth together,
Who likes school dinners anyway?

Lauren Saxty (12)
Kesteven & Grantham Girls' School

TRAGEDY

'Help and shout' are all I can hear,
Children crying, filled with fear.
The once calm, beautiful site,
Is now a scene of war and fight.

The war is becoming deathly and bloody,
From everyone of any nation to see.
Innocent lives are ruined by one,
One bomb, one person, but lives are gone.

Suddenly another bomb I hear,
And I see it dropping like a tear.
What will become of this terrible tragedy?
Why can't these sickened people let it be?

Emma Kirton (13)
Kesteven & Grantham Girls' School

LIGHT

The light that shimmers, glitters, flickers
Through the window on the floor
Fascinates the youngest sibling
Flashing from ceiling to wall.

Light that shines, light that shimmers
Glitters against the dark moonlight
Brightness of a candle flicker
Banishes the dark with light.

Lightning flashes in zigzags
Through the darkness of the sky
Count to when you hear the thunder
Your dear senses never lie.

Star that shines above the world
Looks down upon our lives
Look up and see the past behind
Let them sparkle in your eyes.

The sun that rises in the east
Doth brighten up the day
Light of hope, light of truth
Help us find our way.

Lauren Bland (12)
Kesteven & Grantham Girls' School

THE CONTROLLER

Without me, you would be lost
Bewildered and confused
No one could ever be organised
As I control you.

Without me, there would be no schedules
No breakfast, dinner or supper
No one could ever arrive promptly
As I have control of you.

Without me, there would be no Olympics
As the running would be just a waste
There would be neither a winner, nor a loser
As I have control of you.

As you have guessed, I am quite important
I do control all of your lives
Without me, you could never plan your future
I am *Time.*

Roxanne Croft (13)
Kesteven & Grantham Girls' School

THE TIRING DAY!

I get on the bus at half-past seven,
Even though I'm only eleven.
I get to school in an hour and a bit,
With a bag full of books and PE kit.

After four periods, food is served,
My stomach is rumbling but we have to wait till third.
Scrummy food and delicious treats,
I'll have that and maybe sweets.

Boy, it's been a tiring day,
I just want to get home and then out to play.
It's hard all the homework I have to confess
But I do enjoy KGGS!

I'm on the bus which takes me home,
I'm tired and I want to moan,
About the work I have to do,
So I have written this poem just for you!

Sarah Pope (11)
Kesteven & Grantham Girls' School

WHAT IS THE WORLD?

What is the world?
A place for all living things,
Animals of all different kinds,
A home for me and you,
What is the world?

What is the world?
Rain and snow,
Sun and wind,
Sleet and hail,
What is the world?

What is the world?
A place of war,
A place of peace,
A place of hope and glory,
What is the world?

Joely Ayre (12)
Kesteven & Grantham Girls' School

WEATHER

Rainy days are dull and grey,
The raindrops always seem to spray,
A splash of water in my eyes,
The droplets take you by surprise.

Sunny days are lots of fun,
With hot weather and a big warm sun,
Sometimes you go nice and brown,
But other days make you frown.

Frosty days are cold and slippery,
The frosty air is very nippy,
When it's cold it turns you blue,
We don't care 'cause it's a fun day too.

Snowy days are very white,
The trees and plants are very bright,
It sometimes gives you a nasty burn,
But now it's time for a sunny turn.

Laura Harris (12)
Kesteven & Grantham Girls' School

A BIRTHDAY PARTY

Groovy flowers,
Disco balls,
Flashing lights upon the walls.
Union Jacks hang from the rails,
Balloons float and banners sail.

Cans of Pepsi,
Tons of sweets,
People bopping to the beat.
Funky fashion all the rage,
People dancing on the stage.

Music loud,
Ears ringing,
People join in with the singing.
Happy faces laugh and smile . . .
A birthday party 60s' style!

Jenny Watson (13)
Kesteven & Grantham Girls' School

SEASONS

In spring nature starts to grow,
Animals and plants seem to know,
That it's time to awake from the winter's sleep,
To start collecting their food to keep.

In summer the butterflies and bees come,
And if you sing you will hear the bees hum,
If you listen you will hear the lark sing,
Every day this tune will ring.

In autumn the leaves change their colour,
Things become a lot more duller,
The leaves fall off their trees,
Dancing round in the autumn breeze.

In winter we wrap up warm,
The frost is all over the lawn,
It's time to go back to the winter sleep,
With all the food you've collected to eat.

Winter, spring, summer, autumn,
All the seasons are so awesome,
Frost, flower, bees, leaves,
Are all that come in this time of year.

Bethany Evans (12)
Kesteven & Grantham Girls' School

THE CLANLEY GHOSTS

There was fear in the air,
On our way to Castle Lair,
As we set off on the bus,
Looking forward to a 'just
Especially exhilarating break!'
That's not what we got!

We drove up to the gate,
Ben Parke was sick again,
Our teacher had gone mad,
As the owner's old stepdad,
Invented schooling, education and new life.
You can imagine our strife.

The house was big and burly,
Not at all like Burleigh,
With dragons breathing fire,
Jabbling goblins shouting 'Liar!'
And we wondered if this was some stupid joke,
When our teacher went to get her notes.

We were to wait up on the landing,
Of the largest room still standing,
When overwhelming curiosity broke out.
If we'd had more philosophy we'd doubt,
The Ikea furnished, plush and plurnished bedroom,
When a cowboy ghost came running, gunning out!

From the Mammut-ian wardrobe he came,
And our lovely Mrs Peony he bade,
To come into his stunning lounge.
We were absolutely certain,
As we ran and closed the curtains,
That this house was not a place where we could stay.

The stairs were wrought with fire,
Great crackling flounds of fire,
And a dragon and a lion in its wake,
Were waiting for a single shake
To leap up and eat our life away.

'Oh dear!' we said,
And ran instead
To some well placed loos on the right.
And there began quite a fight
As the boys argued what we would do in the night,
When blobs of jelly, ugly, skrelly toilet ghosts
Began to arise.

So arise did we
And fast did flee,
From the house of the Clanley Dragon
Who nearly stopped poor Hattie on the stairs.
But she dared to undertake a little dare
And snuck the dragon straight out of its lair.

So now the dragon lives not with me,
Or not anymore with anybody,
But never do we mention the day,
When our whole class went to 'play'.
In the house of the Clanley Ghosts.

Rachel Townsend (12)
Kesteven & Grantham Girls' School

for pets
not wanted
side of the road
or life
as.

their own
als or warm firesides
nt to a home
pets are for life
Christmas.

in a cage all day long
to play with or cuddle up to
le walk by without a glance
member, pets are for life
ot just for Christmas.

Why do they do it?
Why don't they care?
Why do they dump us?
Remember, pets are for life
Not just for Christmas.

Bethany Southam (12)
Kesteven & Grantham Girls' School

STARTING SCHOOL

Starting school is always fun
Playing with your nice new friends,
Hoping the day will never end,
Clothes that make you itch,
Talking to your friend Titch,
In music play a quick tune because
Nagging teachers are coming soon.

The corridors are long with so many doors,
Where is my classroom and on which floor?
Can't wait till dinner, hot food now,
Hopefully there won't be cow.

Katherine Spridgens (11)
Kesteven & Grantham Girls' School

THE PERFORMANCE

Trepidation,
Hesitation,
Shivers of excitement,
Why is my mouth so dry,
When my skin is so wet with sweat?

Palpitation,
Jubilation,
Butterflies dancing in my stomach,
Waiting in the wings,
A million images flashing through my head.

Contemplation,
Meditation,
Must focus my mind,
Determined to be good,
After all this time, practise and heartache.

Waiting,
Waiting,
There's my call,
Audience stills,
Exaltation, adoration.

Rebecca Stutely (12)
Kesteven & Grantham Girls' School

THE MOUSE

Crawling quietly, creeping softly,
Along the hall, through the door,
Up the stairs, across the room,
Looking for food, into the drawer.

I've found my treasure and my feast,
Nibbling chocolate, ripping paper,
Out of the drawer, onto the table,
Around the ornaments I caper.

The door creaks open, I turn around,
I run off the table and onto the floor,
Heavy footsteps on the ground,
I think to myself 'Quick, out the door.'

Feeling full, feeling tired,
Down the stairs, I slowly creep,
I've crawled so far, down and down,
I do wish I was asleep!

Into the kitchen I go, round the fridge,
There is a brown box that flapped,
It looks interesting and smells nice too!
I go inside, oh no, *I'm trapped!*

It seems I've been here for hours,
Oh no! I'm moving, where are they taking me?
The air blows in, the box opens!
I'm free, I'm free, *I'm free!*

Katie Baker (12)
Kesteven & Grantham Girls' School

OPEN YOUR EYES

Open your eyes and look around
Look at the golden fields
Touch the rough bark of the trees
Smell the beautiful roses - red, white and yellow
Hear the chattering of the birds.

Open your eyes and look around
Look at the packed shops and traffic jams
Touch the smooth metal lamp posts
Smell the fumes from the bus
Hear the sound of the music from the cars.

Open your eyes and look around
Look at the smiles on the people's faces
Touch the glowing cheeks of a delighted child
Smell the crackling fire in the living room
Hear the laughter of the friends.

Open your eyes and look around
Look at the suffering and hunger
Touch the hand of a dying woman
Smell the smoke of a destructive fire
Hear the sobs of a distraught child.

Open your eyes and look around
Look at the world
Touch, smell and hear
Try to understand.

Anna Butterworth (12)
Kesteven & Grantham Girls' School

HOPE

In a dark, dreary room at the back of my head,
I saw hope,
Like a little candle flame burning away at the black of night,
A way to go when the world blocked me out,
Like praise when everything is dark,
A clear moon on the night of sin,
Like sun on a rainy day,
A ray of hope when the dark was falling,
A person willing to speak their mind when those around them fail,
The ray of hope made shapes on the wall,
Menacing, dark, scary shapes,
They were the shapes my ray of hope made.

Georgina Wade (12)
Kesteven & Grantham Girls' School

THE DAY THE MOON WOKE UP

I looked up at the golden moon,
On a warm autumn afternoon,
I couldn't work out why,
The moon was brightening up the sky.
My dad said, 'The moon is always there,'
I knew he was wrong,
Because earlier, I heard a bird humming a song
And looked up into the sky only to see the sun.
I suddenly remembered what us humans had done,
Earlier today Neil Armstrong walked on the moon.
So I suppose he woke the moon up,
And the moon is still up.

Sophie Smith (11)
Kesteven & Grantham Girls' School

HORROR STORY AT SCHOOL!

In your school you may not think it,
But every school is the same.
All the teachers that work there,
Are completely insane.

Mrs Wigglebottom has a wart on her chin,
And so does Mrs Paine.
On the other hand, Mrs Snipers
Has a permanent migraine.

Why do they give us homework
And always push in the dinner queue,
And write on our work in red pen,
Haven't they got anything else to do?

Lauren Springthorpe (11)
Kesteven & Grantham Girls' School

ANIMALS

Big ones, small ones, some that are in-between.
Fluffy ones, skinny ones, some that are hardly seen.
Woolly, little lambs, cute, fat and sweet,
Underwater animals, I wonder what they eat?

Most animals are nice, but some are quite scary,
And even spiders can be a bit hairy.
Some live in water, some live on farms,
Some even have more than two arms.

Cats and dogs are my favourites
And I like them both the same.
But some animals in the world
Are not quite so tame.

Sarah Plant (11)
Kesteven & Grantham Girls' School

NATURE

Nature is strange
Sometimes it can be surprising

Like getting stung by an angry bee!
Remember to watch quietly
And take care of the countryside.

If you are quiet you could see
Little rabbits in the meadows
Eating the long grass.
When the fox comes by
They run down their holes
Leaving the grass behind them.

You will be aware of the trees in autumn
Their leaves turning from green to red and gold
Squirrels running from branch to branch
And hoarding nuts for the winter.

Louisa Gallimore (11)
Kesteven & Grantham Girls' School

TWENTY POUNDS

Twenty pounds, twenty pounds,
What could I do with that?
I could buy some new clothes and shoes
Or buy my friend's old cat.

Twenty pounds, twenty pounds,
That's quite a lot of money.
I could spend it all on chocs,
But I'd get told off by my mummy.

Twenty pounds, twenty pounds,
That amount could stretch far.
I could save it and in a couple of years
I could buy a flash sports car.

Twenty pounds, twenty pounds,
I know just what I'd do.
I'd invent two money growing trees
And maybe I'd give one to you.

Phoebe Wilcock (11)
Kesteven & Grantham Girls' School

MY ANIMALS

I have three pets,
One rabbit and two guinea pigs.
They live in the garden,
In their hutches.

Flopsy, my oldest pet of all,
Has very long fur which moults once a month.
He loves playing football with his yellow ball,
And compared to my guinea pigs, he is really big.

Cookie, however, who is brown and white,
Has quite rough fur and beautiful eyes.
She loves to chase the other two,
Catching them and cuddling them.

Muffin her sister,
Who is light brown and white,
I think she is the boss,
As she steals all the treats!

Lauren Charles (11)
Kesteven & Grantham Girls' School

MY HOME

In the lounge I sit after school,
Watching TV with my sister,
When my dad comes home from work,
We sit and chat about our day.

In the study I do my homework,
Studying so hard hoping no one will disturb me,
Working so hard, the time passes by,
Then my mum calls me for my tea.

In the kitchen my mum gets the meal,
Working so hard, busy as a bee,
I get out the way and watch the TV,
Until it's time for our lovely tea.

In the dining room I have my tea,
I sit with my family,
We talk about our beautiful day,
And all the exciting things we have done.

After tea I sit in the conservatory,
Relaxing, quiet as can be,
Thinking about the things I have done,
Until it is time to go to bed.

In my bedroom, it's the best of all,
Except for my sister having to share,
I think it has to be,
The best room of all.

Laura Selby (11)
Kesteven & Grantham Girls' School

MY BEST FRIEND

My best friend Jade
Is totally mad
It's not very often
She is sad

She makes me laugh
She makes me smile
She's been my best mate
For such a long while

She is very fit
And likes to run
She especially likes gym
Many trophies she's won

At each other's houses
We sometimes sleep
Having loads of fun
Playing hide-'n'-seek

We stick together
Like super glue
We are always together
In all we do

All in all
My friend Jade
Was one in a million
When she was made.

Emma Pattison (11)
Kesteven & Grantham Girls' School

SCHOOL!

School, what is school?
Mind boggling lessons overpowering my brain.
Questions and answers
Driving me insane.

So now I'm the youngest, a little afraid,
A very large building and many stairs,
Lots of pegs and rows of lockers,
So many classrooms, so many chairs.

Homework, homework more and more,
Some easy, some tough.
It's not as simple as A, B or C,
And three lots of homework is plenty enough.

English and maths
More things to learn and do,
Shapes, lengths and sizes,
Poets and writers too.

Science and history,
Modern and old times to learn about,
Acids and alkalis,
Charges of the horses and a battle cry shout.

PE, PE a mixture of games,
Hockey, netball, gym and dance.
Bats and balls shooting for goal,
I'll do them all and take my chance!

Latin and French
With my little language book.
Trying to learn my foreign alphabet,
New words for there, then and look.

So what is school?
Listening and learning over six hours a day,
Teachers and textbooks, rules and pens.
Will I learn much? Who can say?

Emily Knowles (11)
Kesteven & Grantham Girls' School

SCHOOL UNIFORM

Choosing from the list, what a chore,
I've never known such a fuss before.
Which shop, which street, which town?
Are we going everywhere to choose my gown?

The colours, the styles, the different cloth,
I'll order the tie, that's one thing ticked off.
Time to choose tights or socks,
It really depends which this shop stocks.

The blazer, the badge, the navy blue skirt,
The easiest choice is the pale blue shirt.
Cardigan or jumper, which one is right?
The jumper I think, the cardigan's tight.

Hockey boots, socks and the rest of the kit,
Gym skirts and blouses, the perfect fit.
That's it I think - what do you say?
The only thing left to do is pay.

Alison Askew (11)
Kesteven & Grantham Girls' School

NEW PET

My sister has got a new puppy,
A little springer spaniel.
She's ever so small and cuddly,
Her name is pumpkin.
She plays in the garden,
Exploring, discovering new things all the time.

My mum said last night, Pumpkin was crying,
While she sat on her fleecy pink blanket.
She has settled down a bit now though.

Last night she played in the garden,
I watched her over the wall.
She picked up sticks and ran up banks,
But she didn't play with her ball!

Her little black ears dangle down,
She has loads of black and white hair
All over her little head.
She's got a tiny collar
And the colour of it is bright red.

Joanna Swingler (11)
Kesteven & Grantham Girls' School

MY SCHOOL DAY

7 o'clock in the morning, I'm up with the lark,
Then it's off to school, a walk in the local park.

At registration, they call our names out,
Then it's first lesson with a bright start.

Lunch, it's a break for sandwiches and scones,
The afternoon goes so quickly, it's time to go home.

It's down to dreaded homework,
Which takes me a long time,
Then a bit of TV before it's bedtime.

I close my eyes and I'm out like a spark,
And before I know it, I'm up with the lark.

Megan Abbs (11)
Kesteven & Grantham Girls' School

MY NEW BUNNY, FLICK

I brought him home he looked so funny,
I couldn't believe that I had this bunny.
I wrapped him all up in hay,
I was so very ecstatic that day.

> The next day I named him Flick,
> It was a very hard name to pick.
> As his little beady eyes looked up at me,
> I really wondered what he could see.

He really likes my dog, Lily,
I don't know why, she's quite silly.
He's very soft and very sweet,
My clothes and hair he loves to eat.

> I absolutely love him to bits,
> But he sometimes gets in the biggest fits.
> He likes to get his paws covered in mud
> And when he jumps, you hear a great big thud.

He's extremely handsome and very mad,
I'm not sure if he's got it from his mum or dad.
He makes me feel better when I feel sick
It must be because he's my bunny, *Flick!*

Lucy Moore (11)
Kesteven & Grantham Girls' School

WINTER

Lots of heavy snowing
Pale blue skies
Cold winds blowing
Hot mince pies.

Many misty mornings
White all around
Reports and flood warnings
The crisp, crunchy ground.

People are shivering
Wearing gloves and hats
Trees are quivering
Wet doormats.

Christmas comes
Presents under the tree
Gifts from dads and mums
People laughing happily.

Sat in front of the fire, cosy
As a new layer of snow falls on the ground
Toes are warm, cheeks are rosy
The snow falls without a sound.

Icy cold days
Roaring fires and frosty trees
A misty, cold haze
Many winter memories.

Alice Pullinger (11)
Kesteven & Grantham Girls' School

THE HOUSE

As I walked
up to the door,
inside I saw
the dampest floor.

It was full
with dark green mould
and the atmosphere was
wet and cold.

The curtains they were
ripped and torn
and outside you should
have seen the lawn.

As I opened the door
it gave a squeak
and as I stepped,
I heard a creak.

They ought to get
the cleaners in,
for they don't know
how to use a bin.

You think the owner is
a mouse,
but you are wrong . . .
it is my house!

Olivia Musson (11)
Kesteven & Grantham Girls' School

FEELINGS

Sadness is a feeling,
That some people get,
Sadness is a feeling,
You'd never forget.

Happy is a feeling,
When you smile,
Happy is a feeling,
You'll have for a while.

Loneliness is a feeling,
When you feel left out,
Loneliness is a feeling,
You get quite an amount.

Shyness is a feeling,
When you go all red,
Shyness is a feeling,
You look like you're dead.

Guilt is a feeling,
You feel when you're wrong,
Guilt is a feeling,
Like a copied song.

Love is a feeling,
You actually shine,
Love is a feeling,
You're on cloud number nine.

Sorrow is a feeling,
You have to cry,
Anger is a feeling,
I don't know why.

Feelings are around us every day,
Why oh why do they have to stay?

Joëlle Garland (11)
Kesteven & Grantham Girls' School

HALLOWE'EN

On Hallowe'en night the witches fly
On their broomsticks through the sky.
In the windows pumpkins glow,
Grinning evily row by row.

'Trick or treaters' knock on the door,
They are beginning to annoy me more and more.
Their fancy costumes are so stupid,
I saw one girl dressed up as Cupid.

That night as I lay in bed,
Thoughts are going through my head.
Are there such things as monsters and witches?
If they fall off their broomsticks they'll need some stitches!

I don't believe in ghosts or ghouls
Or things that walk in through the walls.
I don't find all the creatures scary,
Though I'd much prefer them to a fairy.

Then I wake up the next morning
Just as the day is dawning.
On the pavement the stringy stuff looks like worms that are dead,
Why couldn't it be Christmas instead?

Amy Sparks (11)
Kesteven & Grantham Girls' School

WINTER CHILLS

Mist in the morning
Raw and chilly,
Leaves on the pavement
Wet and slippy.

Sun on fire
Behind the trees,
Muddy boots and
Muddy knees!

Shop windows
Lit early,
Soggy grass
Dewy, pearly.

Red, yellow,
Orange and brown,
Silently softly
The leaves float down!

Sophie Adams (12)
Kesteven & Grantham Girls' School

GYM!

Gym, gym, gym
I hate it all the time,
What's the point of gym
When I never win?

Bend and stretch,
Bend and stretch,
Aching all my bones,
The coaches moan
Whenever I groan.

Handstand, handstand,
On my head I land,
The coach wouldn't give me a hand,
So I joined a band!

Katherine Willoughby (11)
Kesteven & Grantham Girls' School

I'VE GOT TO DO MY HOMEWORK

I've got to do my homework
as good as it can be,
or it will say beneath
please see me!

I've got to do my homework
while listening to the noise,
of my stupid little brother
playing with his toys!

I can hear my dad downstairs,
listening to the tele,
he'd better be careful
or he might spill his sherry!

I've got to do my homework
or should I tidy that,
or should I tidy this
or go and feed the cat!

It's time to hand my homework in
I think I've done quite swell,
my teacher's called me over
and said I did well!

Sophie Elgar (11)
Kesteven & Grantham Girls' School

THE DAYS OF THE WEEK

I do not know
The days of the week
I wish, I wish, I wish
That to me they would speak.

I know I'll try and learn
A rhyme!
Then the days of the week
Shall be mine!

Today is tomorrow
Tomorrow is today
Because tomorrow
Swapped places with yesterday.

No! No! No!

I think yesterday got jealous
Of today
And forced him to sway
With tomorrow.

No! No! No!

I think tomorrow got angry
And wanted to swap
With Tuesday next week
But Wednesday cried 'Stop.'

No! No! No!

Don't get me mixed up
It's hard enough to learn
The days of the week
Just my luck.

Now stop it
Monday, Tuesday, Wednesday,
Thursday, Friday, Saturday,
Yes and you, Sunday!

Yes, yes, I did it!
I said them all together!
I will know them now
For ever and ever and ever!

Fiona McLaughlin (11)
Kesteven & Grantham Girls' School

DINNER LADIES

The dinner ladies sit and scowl
And wipe their nose on some kitchen towel
Their greasy hair
And awful glare
Which could give you quite a dreadful scare

Their aprons are smeared
In grease and slime
And serving dinners takes them
An awful long time

Their fingernails are filled with gunk
And the kitchen full of horrendous junk
We all leave the dinner hall
And all you can hear is an echoing moan
After three hours of moaning they all go *home!*

Grace Costello (12)
Kesteven & Grantham Girls' School

SEASONS

Summer

Summer days are hot,
The sun is shining,
There's no cloud in sight,
People are bathing, swimming
And having fun,
Then it ends and autumn is here.

Autumn

When the trees are bare
The leaves hit the ground
And the wind whistles by
And sweeps them about,
Then the trees are bare,
Then it ends and winter is here.

Winter

Out come the gloves, hats and scarves,
The freezing cold wind blows,
People standing, freezing cold
While snowmen are being built,
Then it ends and spring is here.

Spring

It is mild and
All the lambs and calves
And other animals are born.
Blossom on the tree is pink and white,
Then it ends and the seasons start again.

Danielle Winters (12)
Kesteven & Grantham Girls' School

FOREVER

The relaxation, the sounds of peace!
The blazing sunset, the open air,
The hills of green grass
And the cliffs of grey rocks.

Floating
Calm, tranquil, floating on air,
Voices not to be heard.
The sound is no more!

Imagine
Trees, bushes, branches, seas!
Quiet as the world.
God's world, his life, his home!
The pain, the hunger, the wars
Are no more!

Silence
No one suffers, no one fears,
It all seems to go.
People aren't heard,
Noises are extinct,
Silence is the king!

Peace
The fears stop,
People stop,
Sounds stop,
But the Earth goes on
Forever!

Heidi Maclachlan (11)
Kesteven & Grantham Girls' School

SCHOOL

My first day at high school was really scary,
As my teacher was really hairy.
The second day was not too bad,
As my maths teacher went mad.

The third day I was sick of school,
As I was the biggest fool.
The fourth day I was giving up
And felt like smashing a cup.

The fifth day was going wrong,
As I said, 'Keep your hair on.'
The sixth day I got into the swing
And cried aloud, 'I'm the king.'

Three weeks on, it's not too bad,
I'm sure now I'm going mad.
Homework, homework all the time,
It's hard to get to bed for nine.

Up again and off we go,
Homework, school, to and fro.
Now let's think it won't be long,
Till my school days have all gone.

Sarah Toulson (12)
Kesteven & Grantham Girls' School

SKIING

Cold, fresh, mountain air
No mist, but a bright sun.
It's a great day to ski
But first the bakery for a bun.

Go down to the lockers
Get out your skis,
But you have to be careful putting them on
So as not to fall on your knees.

Go and catch the chairlift
Up into the sky,
But be careful for your first time
Or on your back you'll lie.

Swishing from side to side
Making the snow shoot up
Stopping off at a bar
Drinking hot chocolate from a cup.

Time to head back
Put the skis away
Have some French tea
Then nine card brag is what we play
And tomorrow the day starts again.

Charlotte Cleveland (11)
Kesteven & Grantham Girls' School

WHAT KIND OF PET SHALL I GET?

What kind of pet shall I get?
Dogs obviously cost a lot, I bet,
Cats can be vicious but a really nice pet,
Mice, hmm, a white one, I've met.

Lots of animals I'll lose count,
Naughty monkeys I'll have to rant,
Spiders, scorpions, or even an ant,
Or maybe I'll buy an elephant.

I don't know how I will decide,
Buying a horse would be a ride,
If I bought a swan it would get lost in the tide,
If I bought a gerbil I would need a guide.

Animals can come from far away,
Coming to me on this very day,
Like dragons I might not have to pay,
Dragons come from over the sea at the bay.

Farmyard animals like a chicken,
Woodland animals like a woodpecker pecking,
Buffalo in the house, they'd be wrecking.
Back to dogs, they wouldn't stop licking.

How about sea creatures like a manta ray?
Aww, how sweet I would say.
If it is a very hot day,
All the rays would go to the shade to stay.

All these different animals to choose,
Like Noah said, they go in twos.
If I don't hurry I will lose,
What kind of pet shall I choose?

Michelle Lee (11)
Kesteven & Grantham Girls' School

WIND EASE

The sound of the wind howling in my ear comforts me
in the meadows.
It relaxes me as I lay staring at the clouds,
Watching the shapes changing into many mysterious
forms.
I feel a great sensation as the wind blows.
It tingles my body, sending shivers down my back.
The rain beats down, being blown to me,
Like the spray of waves crashing against the rocks.
I feel so good, in my own little world,
Dreaming and concentrating,
On my wonderful engagement with life.

Nathan Cock (14)
Middlecott School

MY FAMILY

My family are really cool,
Especially my brother who acts like a fool.
My dad's head is quite small,
But then again he's very tall.
As for my mum, she sings at night,
It gives us all a fright,
She makes a loud din,
Which makes us shout
And run about,
But the best thing is that they are always there.

Kathryn Brewster (12)
Middlecott School

FOUR SEASONS

Winter
It's the middle of winter
But where's the snow?
The sun has gone
But not for long.

Spring
The sun is now here
The trees are blooming
Birds are nesting
But no snow.

Summer
The sun is hotter than ever
I'm hot and bothered
But it's my birthday
I'm still really hot.

Autumn
There's not much sun
But there is a cold breeze
Birds fly south
But I can't
I've got no wings.

Linzee Vickers (12)
Middlecott School

DOLPHINS

I love to watch the dolphins glide,
Tails flipping from side to side,
Beneath the ocean spray they hide.

My dream one day would be to swim,
Holding tightly to its fin.
Bluey-grey, velvet skin,
With my favourite mammal, a dolphin.

Zoe Whitworth (12)
Middlecott School

A MONDAY EXPERIENCE

Queuing last night in the rain,
At the time seemed such a pain.
I had gone with my mum to look,
At Jacqueline Wilson sign her new book.

The people had come from afar,
Such popularity is bizarre.
We snaked along the street,
Moving so slowly, shuffling our feet.

People kept coming out of the shop,
Saying you really are mad to stop.
Wait until you get inside and see,
At least another hour you will be.

Apparently Jacqueline Wilson is such fun,
So much to say, especially to all the mums.
Her hands are covered in rings,
She's quite happy to sign anything you bring.

Then my headache began,
Suddenly I didn't feel such a fan.
My mum said perhaps we should give up and go,
Now this famous lady I shall never know.

Joe Roberts (12)
Middlecott School

DT

I think DT is great
Mr Daley
Is my mate.

Metalwork's cool
Because we don't
Sit on a stool.

Plastic work is the same
But I think it's really
Lame.

Woodwork gives me a smirk
Because I have to
Work.

Jonathan Storey (12)
Middlecott School

CRUELTY TO ANIMALS

Cruelty to animals
is not very fair.
Don't get them in the first place
if you can't treat them with care.
Don't trap their tails in the door
or you will make them cry for sure.
Don't tread on their little toes
or kick them on their little nose.
If you get fed up with them
don't throw them away,
just pick up the telephone
and call the RSPCA!

Charlene Blakey (13)
Middlecott School

LOVE YOU!

I love the way you gel your hair,
And the way it just falls down,
I love it when you come outside
And the way you hang around.
I love it when you cuddle me
And the way you say my name,
I love the way you look at me,
I've got your picture in my frame.
I hate it when we argue
And the way you think I stare,
But the truth is I do like you
And you know I do,
And you know I will always care.

Vicki Taylforth (12)
Middlecott School

PE

PE, PE, PE is great,
PE helps me lose weight,
Mr Chester is my mate,
The things we do are great.

PE, PE, PE is fun,
All the things we have done!
Broken bones, grazed knees,
I have done all these.

All these I have done,
PE is fun!

Rory Young (12)
Middlecott School

LAUGHED OUT LOUD

I laughed out loud
everybody stopped and stared,
giving me dirty looks as they glared.
I felt I'd done something terrible . . .
but what?
I started to shake
like an earthquake.
All I could think was - why?
What had I done wrong
to deserve the attention of this staring throng?
I felt I'd been caged -
a strange looking animal at the zoo.
I felt so tiny - the size of an ant.
My self-esteem was so low.
But why? All I'd done was laugh out loud.

Katy Lamb (14)
Queen Elizabeth's High School

WHO I AM

I am a swirly, purpley-blue, glittering like a diamond.
I am the sweet smell of bluebells swaying in the breeze.
I am the fluffy feel of a purple cushion topped with pearls.
I am the taste of melted chocolate, wrapped around a silky centre.
I am the sight of a disco ball whose reflection dances on the wall.
I am a blue whale swimming majestically in the blue ocean.
I am the sound of heavenly chimes, tinkling in the wind.
I am the beach of Miami, basking in the sun.
I am a juicy, red strawberry sitting amid the leaves, ready to be picked.
I am a squeaky clarinet just learning to be played.

Hannah Norton (11)
Queen Elizabeth's High School

WHAT A MORN!

What a morn!
We wake up to hear
We want what we don't want to see
The terrorist has struck
We see a plane
A plane that was forced to crash
Innocent lives have been taken
Why oh why God let this happen?
Fear has struck
Smoke flames bellow out of buildings
Screams we hear
Some loud, some faint
What has happened to the world
A world once thought safe
A time not to be repeated
People frantic in the streets
Shouts of help from those who are injured
Lost souls buried in rubble
Never to be seen again
Why oh why did God let this happen?
Clothing, shoes strewn on the wayside
Dust and smoke choke you to death
Distended lights bellow through
Sirens come and the go
What a bloody day from the USA.

Drew Bowness (13)
Queen Elizabeth's High School

WEEP NO MORE

She helped you fight back through the rough, bad times,
Now she's gone, you do not know what else to do.
She was your voice when you could not speak,
She made you strong when you were weak,
All you seem to do is curl up and weep.

There was a reason why God took her away,
But maybe you weren't meant to comprehend.
She lived life joyously and to the full,
Life doesn't have a meaning but it still goes on.

Glowing in the darkness, she leads your life,
She was your hero then she departed this world.
Though she is gone, she's in your heart for evermore.

It's time to start healing from the pain you have,
You know she's merry and safe in her life above.

Goodbye and God bless for evermore.

Angela Chan (13)
Queen Elizabeth's High School

A TALE OF TWO TOWERS

The towers soar way up high,
As if about to pierce the sky.
The towers are filled to the top,
From the peak it's an immense drop.

The plane collides into the tower,
It gives the terrorists lots of power.
The planes harboured kamikaze,
The towers people begged for mercy.

As the first tower fell,
There was an artificial hell.
Now thousands are dead,
Given an early deathbed.

In the wreck are people's lovers,
Children, fathers, daughters and mothers,
The towers stood tall and strong,
Apparently we all were wrong.

Steve Robinson (14)
Queen Elizabeth's High School

I AM . . .

I am the bright yellow sun,
intertwined with an array of glistening orange gems.

I am the sweet smell of roses, flourishing freely.

I am silk, sleek, soft and smooth,
gliding gracefully across glistening skin.

I am a musical sweet sounding songbird
chanting in a chestnut tree.

I am a tangy and zesty, juicy lemon.

I am a cat sleeping, lazily yet as fast as lightning.

I am a dainty dancer, gracefully twisting and turning,
lunging and leaping.

I am a cheetah sprinting speedily, across the plain.

I am the wind whipping up the waves.

Katie Shepherd (12)
Queen Elizabeth's High School

I NEED A REASON

Only tears of sadness go to those who die,
Only cries of joy go to those who live,
But what cry goes to those who are stuck?
What cry goes to those who help?
And what cry goes to those who wait?
Only through the eyes of the witnesses do we know what happened.
Only through the eyes of the suspect do we know why it happened.
Only through the eyes of the dead do we know the suffering.
Only through the eyes of the stuck do we know where we are.
Only one person knows why it happened, why?

Claire Stringer (12)
Queen Elizabeth's High School

WAR

With a bang the bullet flies,
With a thud the victim dies.
The Russian tanks, a city shelled,
The assassin's gun, another man felled.
An unexploded landmine, waiting in the sand
And in time on it a child will stand.
The guided missile, another plane downed,
A torpedoed sub, many men drowned.
The mighty cruise missiles find their mark,
A raging inferno started by a spark.
An artillery shell lands with a thud,
Many men lay still in the mud.
Can't we see that war is just death, bloodshed and pain
And that we should stop it from happening ever again?

Stewart Simpkins (14)
Queen Elizabeth's High School

MAJORCAN EVENING

Black silhouettes on the golden autumn leaves
In the sunset reflected in the sea.
Motionless waves, sunbeams dancing
Calmly, silently gushing up the beach,
Covering my feet then sweeping back again,
Revealing my feet once more a shiny wet gleam on them.
The lonely beach, everything silent
Apart from the gentle murmuring in the background
From contented couples,
The buzzing lunch bars along the sea front now remain empty.
The lights on the harbour front gleam like the silent moon,
Gently drifting in the unknown deep sky with no destination.
The reflection distorted like a silent ghost gleaming on the sea's edge.
The golden sand lay still until the morn.

Vicky McIlroy (14)
Queen Elizabeth's High School

ONE PERSON'S VOICE

I was the look of silk,
I was the fairies, flowing frills,
I was a strawberry waiting to be eaten,
I was the scent of freshly cut grass,
I was a delicate, dancer's dream,
I was the wittering wind whispering through ears,
I was a tall, slender lily,
I was the leap from white to pink,
I was a field of lilies swaying,
I am now the soil's earth.

Harriet Tully (14)
Queen Elizabeth's High School

I Am . . .

I am a light blue day with a speckle of clouds bouncing about,
I am the rough texture of clambered rocks,
I am a bacon buttie sizzling in the morning,
I am the splashing of water racing down the waterfall,
I am the dark moonlight sparkling,
I am a loud shirt dazzling brightly out of the rest,
I am an ant always moving, never stood still,
I am a hardcore listener which is connected to hardcore music
And a drummer beating his sticks to the drums
till they've fallen to pieces.

I am . . .

Alex Lee (12)
Queen Elizabeth's High School

Who Am I?

I am pink with crashes of purple,
I am smooth waves,
I am the scent of sweet roses,
I am the sound of my breathing, gently pounding,
I am a pink panther with extended legs,
I am the sweet taste of chocolate,
I am a fickle chameleon, changing colour in the sun,
I am a singing bird, high in the trees,
I have long, silky, black hair like a horse.
Who am I?

Benazir Mungur (12)
Queen Elizabeth's High School

A Tribute To My Guinea Pig, Spicy

Your fur is black as the night
and ginger like glowing embers of a fire.
Your eyes glitter like a mirrorball at a disco,
you chirrup and squeak when you are happy.
When I see you nibbling at the grass in your run,
it makes me smile.
When I rub my hand along your back,
you purr like the engine of a moped.
I love the way you jump and run around in the lounge,
occasionally poking your head around the sofa.
You make me feel safe
and when I'm scared, I talk to you.
I can tell you all my problems and share all my secrets with you.
I know you won't tell anyone.
When you want my attention, you nuzzle my arm.
You seem to grin when I kiss you goodnight
and return the favour by licking my nose.
Life just wouldn't be the same if you weren't there.

Laura Ogley (14)
Queen Elizabeth's High School

I Am . . .

I am a pattern of lime-green and orange.
I am a strawberry sensation, weaving through the air.
I am a hot and spicy chilli, sprinkled with Parmesan cheese.
I am a smooth rock worn down by the sea.
I am a bird singing in the highest of trees.
I am the steepest of hills turning into a valley so deep.
I am a sea horse swimming near the warm shores
And mingling with the seaweed.
I am an eagle soaring through the cloudless skies.

Hannah Espin (11)
Queen Elizabeth's High School

THE WORLD STOOD STILL

The eleventh of September, two thousand and one,
An ordinary autumn day.
People busy, rushing to work,
Oblivious of what was to come.

In the minds of others,
Evil thoughts prevailed
Thoughts set to motion,
The nightmare began . . .

A scene of carnage,
Of fire, smoke and dust.
Of tears, terror and torment,
The memories will haunt millions.

The pain, the hate and the sorrow,
The loss of innocent lives.
A country that weeps,
Shattered, broken.

The world united in grief,
But love and hope continue . . .

Sophie Bryant (16)
Queen Elizabeth's High School

GRANDAD

It was three years ago in July,
My grandad passed away,
But because I was unaware,
It was like any other day.

But when my mum told me
What had really happened,
I realised all the things
I hadn't said.

I hardly ever spoke to him,
Because I was out playing,
But those few conversations
Were amazing.

Sarah Emara (14)
Queen Elizabeth's High School

ELEPHANT

Parading across the wild African plain,
the most enormous thing you've ever seen.

It's the elephant, one of the most beautiful
and magnificent creatures ever to be.

He tramples on everything in his path,
as though a bulldozer crushing concrete.

His trunk can do a thousand things,
that makes his life so worthwhile.

As he bathes in the mud in the heat of the day,
his fellow companions join him.

His ears are like portable fans,
cooling him from the fire of the sun.

Those extremely sharp tusks warn off any
enemy from the animal kingdom.

Unfortunately they don't warn off poachers
who kill them for their ivory.

At the end of the day, as dusk draws near,
the elephant retires,
to the shelter and security of the undergrowth.

Kimberley Aukland (14)
Queen Elizabeth's High School

A City Drowned In Tears

The sky is blackened
Fire fills the air
Thousands are killed
This can't be fair.

The world is silent
Shock fills every heart
This godless act
Has torn their lives apart.

People pray
Their relatives lost
They have suffered
The largest cost.

Denial and confusion
They just can't cope
Though amongst the terror
Emerges hope.

Strength is gathered
Like never before
The heroes are working
Until they can work no more.

Although they work hard
The skyline is clean
And tears have flooded
This city of dreams.

Chris Bryant (14)
Queen Elizabeth's High School

MUSIC IS MY LIFE

Music has always played a big part in my life.
Styles like rap, garage, pop, RnB, classical are just a few.
Each type has their own sound expressing moods and feelings.
Music can help change a person's life.
It can make a depressed person look at the cloud
and see the silver lining.

Music has influenced me in so many ways.
Even from when I was young, I can remember playing an instrument.
Happy tunes cheer me up, and I want to share that feeling
with everyone.
Playing the saxophone helps me to release stress and express
my emotions.
I get such a buzz when I play for a crowd, words can't describe.

Music creates a mood which is used for special occasions.
For weddings a happy tune is played, for funerals the opposite.
Every person enjoys a different type of music and many music
artists have become idols.
To the extent of posters filling rooms and money used to buy CDs.
One particular song can win the heart of someone special.

Everywhere you go some form of music is heard.
Whether it's the wind howling or the bird's chirping.
Craig David blasting out of his fans' windows, or the sound
of car exhausts polluting our world.
Music is everywhere and there is no escape.
Luckily for me though, I love music and it can follow me everywhere.

Alison Towning (14)
Queen Elizabeth's High School

STALKER

I look behind me,
He moves closer,
Fear in my eyes,
Tears streaming down my face,
Harsh eyes, staring, a bright white,
Sharp silver skin glistening in the moonlight,
Running from him,
I stumble,
Fall into the mud,
Look again he's closer,
Rain trickling down my face,
Upon me he stands,
Breathing heavily down my neck,
Shut my eyes and pray to wake up.

Alex Smith (14)
Queen Elizabeth's High School

ME

I am a madman searching for adrenaline
Rushing past things
Bright flashes of green and orange.

> I am daring, living life on the edge
> Yet calm and collected when I want to be
> I am a lizard in the desert
> Exploring new territories.

I am a sweet tooth
I am daring and risky
This is me.

Tom Lewis (12)
Queen Elizabeth's High School

THE WORLD THROUGH MY EYES

Colourful surroundings
Evil just makes me want to scream
Hatred seems to rule the world
I'm no angel
I do bad things and make mistakes
I'm only human after all.
I work hard trying to achieve
My greatest dream
To become a programmer
Help others
Who cannot help themselves
When it comes to computers
I want to be the best
Achieve what no one else has.

Adam Middleton (14)
Queen Elizabeth's High School

ME, MYSELF AND I

I am bluey-purple swirls covered with green glitter.
I am the aromatic spices of a hot curry.
I am chewy, gooey, sweet, sticky caramel.
I am the serene and majestic swan gliding on the water.
I am the velvety skin on a juicy, plump peach.
I am the dawn chorus of morning birds.
I am the golden Labrador - faithful and obedient to their master.
I am a bowling ball hitting ten pins.
I am a duck floating on water
I am the sunset after a hot, balmy day.

Heidi Bartle (11)
Queen Elizabeth's High School

I AM...

I am the centre yellow of the shining sun.
I am the soft golden sand on the uneven shore.
I am the sweet taste of melted chocolate.
I am the compact gentleness of an ant.
I am the sound of a tiny bird chirping high in the trees.
I am a mini chugging round a cross-country course.
I am shark fish swimming a great distance in the shimmering pool.
I am the natural smell of the woodland.
I am the cushiony lining of the bright, white clouds high in the sky.

Laura Saxelby (12)
Queen Elizabeth's High School

RETURN

Strangers in a crowded room,
Deathly silent,
Quiet as a tomb,
Energy buzzing, alight in the air,
Waiting,
For the door to open,
Anticipating,
The looming moment,
It's been so long,
Separated by oceans,
Felt horribly wrong,
To be apart,
A flash of green as they walk through,
Watching closely,
For the one you knew,
Droves and droves in uniform.

Lynne Coleman (16)
Queen Elizabeth's High School

DREAMLAND

A perfect land,
Fantastic scenery all around,
Everything you want it to be,
Your dreamland.

The guy of your dreams,
The most supreme moment ever!
The dreams you want to dream again,
Or dreams you are pleased to wake up from.

Amazing and fantastic,
Or shadowy and frightening,
You never know what you will dream,
You just lay there, in bed and think,
'What will happen tonight
In Dreamland?'

Megan Cumberland (13)
Queen Elizabeth's High School

ME

I am a patch of green grass, bright and cheerful.
I am a smooth silky knife but my blade can be sharp.
I am a daisy with a sweet soft gentle scent.
I am a voice singing to someone's heart.
I am a cheeky monkey with a few tricks my sleeves.
I am a sweet orange but I can be a sour lemon.
I am a free bird flying where I please.
I am a competitor in the world's adventure course.
I am a porcelain doll, easily broken.
I am a simple person in a complicated world.

Chloe Ashwell (12)
Queen Elizabeth's High School

UNTITLED

Innocent bodies everywhere,
Someone's mother, father, brother, sister and child,
Obliterated and killed.
For what?
Death of thousands and no reason why.
A bloodbath of innocent souls.
An occasional cry from the darkness below,
Hope is still there.
Flowers are black,
Clouds dull,
Not even an single ray of light shines.
Who benefits from all these atrocities?
A tragedy affecting everybody,
A nightmare for life.
Yesterday it was Palestine and Israel,
Today America,
Tomorrow the world.

Yakut Khan (14)
Queen Elizabeth's High School

ME?

I am twists of enchanting lilac and lime,
I am a smooth knife, though my blade can be sharp.
I am a bouquet of roses, in all shapes and sizes.
I am a soft sounding violin.
I am a peg, holding many things together.
I am chocolate ice cream, sweet but eat me wrong and I'm cold.
I am a lazy cat, but affectionate and cuddly.
I am wild horse, carefree and running where I please.
I am a flower, I grow with space, time and plenty of care.
I am whatever I feel, anything I think, anyone I meet.

Laura Hulley (13)
Queen Elizabeth's High School

WHAT AM I?

I am a deep ocean and midnight blue, glittering with stars and
                                    reflection of the moon.
I am dark, rich and mint caramel chocolate with a hint
                                    of strawberry.
I am a luxurious piece of silky velvet with some light creases.
I am a whisper in the trees and a crunching of leaves.
I am flowing and easy to look at but not so easy to see.
I am a sleeping dragon, calm and cool.
I am a book, old and mysterious and not very easy to read.
I am more interesting when you have finished my book and
                                    understand it.
I am not always myself.

Christina Brown (12)
Queen Elizabeth's High School

SURFING

As I enter the water
the anticipation is mounting
to find the biggest wave
just waiting, waiting, waiting.
Then out of nowhere
a wave was starting
climbing, climbing, climbing,
people stuttering, spluttering
of the height of the wave.
It seemed to stay there, motionless.
Suddenly the archway starts to form,
the froth of the wave pushes everyone
back to the shore, and ending
with a hissing noise on the bay.

Matthew Shanks (13)
Queen Elizabeth's High School

DIFFERENT WORLD, SAME DREAM

Sitting, uninvited in the corner,
Hidden by my own cloud of solitude,
Looking through unknown eyes at the scene before me,
Laughter and unity filling every nook and cranny in the room.
Friends, lovers, admirers . . . something I will never have,
My life desire is . . . to be popular and known as 'the one'
To have people surrounding me with happiness and loyalty
                                        I can share.
Waving, talking and watching me stride down the corridor,
Ruler of the whole teenage population
Princess of Popularity,
The real me not shown to others, only to myself,
And I wonder, 'Is this true?'
Maybe it is, doubts cross my mind.
And I realise, that my desire in life has come true,
At a time of need, this life I have now received
Is not what it is thought to be,
But, is in my dream . . .

Alice Rodgers (14)
Queen Elizabeth's High School

I AM . . .

I am stripes of orange and red with flashes of gold.
I am the cold smell of morning dew resting on the grass.
I am the rich sweet taste of chocolate melting on your tongue.
I am a silky touch of a soft cream wedding dress.
I am a whistling sound of early birds high up in the trees.
I am a glittering sight of a shining silver ring.
I am a beautiful unicorn flying gracefully away.
I am a dark pool of water deep in the centre of your eye.
I am a smile dancing widely on someone's face.

Maddie Dixon (12)
Queen Elizabeth's High School

THROUGH MY EYES ONLY

As a baby, newborn and innocent
I am bright orange flecked with maroon,
I am roses tinting of lily,
I am thick, golden, gooey syrup,
I am smooth, flat silk,
I am a jovial flute concerto,
I am an open box who never shuts,
I am a robin chick, depending on others for help,
I am a darting flapping butterfly, chasing the wind.

Growing up, not so innocent, learning, changing.
I am tie-dye purple, patching up over old things,
I am freshly mown grass, sweet and plentiful,
I am chocolate, hinting disguised flavours,
I am satin with prominent, rough creases,
I am sad, quiet, mournful piano piece,
I am long, sweeping, drawn curtain that nobody can open,
I am a wolf, moving in numbers for safety,
I am a megaphone, heard above everything.

As I am now, wiser, more sensible and still changing.
I am vibrant pink, splattered with blood-red,
I am fresh magnolia suggesting lime zest,
I am sweet sugar lumps, melting into rich, black coffee,
I am wrinkled, strong velvet,
I am loud, steady drum beats
I am black rain cloud, but, whitening every day,
I am a solitary, defensive hedgehog,
I am a CD playing loud rock songs day and night.

Charlotte Binstead (11)
Queen Elizabeth's High School

I Am What I Am

I am a yellow sun on a hot summer's day,
I am long, wavy, golden corn at harvestime,
I am a cat curled up tight in front of a warm, hot fire,
I am a rabbit hopping around and playing all day,
I am the sound of wind chimes jingling in the warm breeze,
I am the patter of rain splishing and sploshing in puddles,
I am a woodland walk twisting and turning past giant waterfalls
and ponds,
I am the countryside away from the hustle and bustle of city life,
I am a smooth, shiny crystal glimmering in the light,
I am a bouncy, springy bed that children jump and play on,
I am a piece of yellow cheese with holes which mice like to nibble,
I am some chewy delicious meat that gets stuck in your teeth,
I am the smell of a brand new book,
I am the smell of fresh paint as you open the large metal tin,
I am a computer memory,
I am a mad, crazy golf course,
I am the beautiful Lake District that everyone wants to see,
I am Gelert the dog, in the legend from Wales,
I am a soft, springy, warm sofa that gets to relax all day,
I am a technological, terrific television that's tuneable to tiny thoughts.

Daniel Price (13)
Queen Elizabeth's High School

Through The Eyes Of Myself

I am a deep, dark blue with swirls of white.
I am the blazing sun setting mystically across the horizon.
I am the sound of the ocean waves splashing against the ridged rocks.
I am the touch of soft, sleek velvet.
I am the smell of early, fresh morning time.

I am the taste of a sour grapefruit covered with sweet sugar.
I am an elegant dolphin diving peacefully in the waves.
I am a delicate and graceful ballet dancer in spotlight on the stage.
I am a complicated book pages and pages long.
I am a cool gentle breeze in the quiet evening.

Amy Cuthbert (11)
Queen Elizabeth's High School

WHY?

Why? Why the Pentagon?
  Why the towers?
Why the relations that were ours?

Why? Why that father?
  Why that mother?
  Why that sister?
  Why that brother?

Why? Why now?
  When everything seemed to be going well!
  This was a pure act just from hell!

This, this can't be just a cry for help and attention -
  Can it?

If, if I'm dreaming, I don't like this dream, more like a
                              nightmare unfortunately.

And, and if we had a minute's silence for each life lost

We, we would be here forever living in a very quiet world.

Jennifer Crow (12)
Queen Elizabeth's High School

IMPACT

The morning mist lay dormant
over death and destruction.
The once unstoppable Trade Centre,
New York's character and landmark,
were hit today by terrorists.
Thousands of civilian lives, just slaughtered.
The first impact they thought was an accident
But the second,
No way!
The 11th September 2001
will stay with us forever.
A day of pain and disaster.
Every corner of the world grieves.
It's not meant to be like this.
Please find pain and sorrow in your heart
and let there be justice.

Jemma Leese (13)
Queen Elizabeth's High School

ME

I am the deafening roar of Michael Owen's goal.
I am a sour, yellow lemon.
I am freshly squeezed orange juice.
I am a spotted cheetah sprinting through the sandy desert.
I am a clean, shiny, new white football.
I am the rooster as he coasts round the buoy.
I am clothes, fresh off the line.
I am a bright blue, fresh morning sky.
I am Ian Wilkinson as he pulls a perfect layout.
I am the kiss that meets the cheek.

Rebecca Lee (13)
Queen Elizabeth's High School

WHO AM I?

I am pink and purple stripes, bright, cheerful and glitzy.
I am soft as silk in the day, but rough and ready in the mornings.
I am a newly budded rose, among an orchard of flowers.
I am a songbird, chirping away at dawn.
I am the Statue of Liberty, willing to give everybody freedom.
I am the taste of a cherrybomb sweet, too hot to handle.
I am a puppy, cuddly and soft.
I am a model, upon a dazzling stage.
I am a footballer, whizzing across an open, muddy field.
I am a new book, with a shiny and glossy front cover.
But most importantly, I am me, and that's who I want to be . . .

Amy Edwards (12)
Queen Elizabeth's High School

WHAT I AM

I am splashes of blue and yellow topped with a tinge of green.
I am smooth but with patches of rust on a sheet of metal.
I am sweet and sharp, as sea air.
I am twinkling and sprinkling; a small water fountain, with a
                                        stone lion in the centre.
I am flowers in a park, many different colours.
I am sherbet lemon, sweet and tangy.
I am a shark, making masses of bubbles when swimming in water.
I am a football, flying round the pitch.
I am a pot of glue, sticky and tacky.
I am a bee, busy and lazy.

Jeremy West (12)
Queen Elizabeth's High School

MEMORIES

As I sit in my class
I listen to the teacher drone on,
When I gaze out the window I see
A place where I would rather be.
A field of lush green grass and trees,
People playing gleefully.
When I gaze into my memory I see
A small wood with young thin trees,
The autumn leaves fall all around
And rustle as they hit the ground.
Me and my friends play
Running through tall uncut grass,
We were free without walls.
As reality creeps back in
I see how we are all penned in
By rules and white washed walls.
How I long to be back with the falling leaves
Weaving carefree through the trees.

Alex McLeod (13)
Queen Elizabeth's High School

IN A DIFFERENT WAY

I am a purple night sky with silver shooting stars.
I am a porcelain doll with perfect brunette curls.
I am a pair of silk curtains hanging in the window.
I am a sweet tooth for chocolate.
I am a lion prowling around, guarding my territory.
I am a violin playing its sweet slow tune.
I am a field of poppies growing up, bursting with colour.
I am a sharpened down pencil writing a long story.
I am a great novel constantly being picked up.

Michaela Lagdon (11)
Queen Elizabeth's High School

CRACKLING WONKA BAR

I am a purple swirl glimmering in the sun,
I am a bottlenose dolphin making a lot of noise,
I am tuna and sweetcorn squished into sliced, white bread
for sandwiches,
I am a tweeting bird waking everybody up in the morning,
I am the texture of soft, spongy dough waiting to be risen.
I am the scent of burning candles in the middle of the table.
I am a shiny fish with a hook in my mouth.
I am a gold pound coin shimmering in a denim jean pocket.
I am a crackling Wonka Bar exploding in someone's mouth.
I am knight's shining armour, rescuing all the ladies.

Rhianne Elway (11)
Queen Elizabeth's High School

RAIN

Rain is a pain,
It slows you down
And you never know,
You could drown.

It comes in different colours
And is also very cold.
It comes in hailstones,
I bet you'll get wet.

Some people like it,
I don't mind,
Some people don't like it,
How do you find it?

Lucie Birkett (13)
Queen Elizabeth's High School

THE 11TH SEPTEMBER 2001

Smash
rocks crumbling
windows smashing
bricks falling
rubble dominating
borders lost
boundaries forgotten

Destruction
flames darting
ashes spitting
fire spreading
embers remain in a dying fire

Devastation
pain
suffering
terror
fright
misery
death

Torture
deliberate, sick mass slaughter
the sorcerer shows no remorse and regrets nothing
the demon sits back, laughs and admires his work.

Ben Langdale (14)
Queen Elizabeth's High School

IF ONLY

The referee sounds his whistle
And the phantom fans start chanting
The fly half steps up to take the kick
And fifteen ugly men run at you.

The fields are getting muddy
And rain is pouring down
Hopefully full time won't be too long
Partying and drinking getting closer.

The first pass you get you drop
And teammates' heads go down in dismay
A high kick comes your way
You catch it and you're on the run.

You speed past two
Dummy past another
Side step four
And over the tryline you go.

It looks as if time is nearly up
Fans blowing horns and whistles
St George of England
Are again beating the Scottish thistle.

The referee sounds his whistle for full time
Players shake hands and replace shirts
You wake up in a sweat
Thinking . . . if only!

Tom Barnett (13)
Queen Elizabeth's High School

The Big Apple

A distant phone ringing,
disaster: lies, undiscovered.
A child in the street crying,
fearing a loved one dead.

In a far off land many cheer,
praise the deed of the martyr.
For no one do they fear.

A thought to the shattered lives,
of those brave and loving spirits.
Relations, nations, close become, allies.
Think of those now lost to a place of bliss.

Darkness falls over the white blanket,
nothing compares to an annihilation so tragic.

Lauren Fulcher (16)
Queen Elizabeth's High School

Grandad

He is a word puzzle, a difficult crossword, a book of knowledge.
He's an ant, making something every day.
He's a fork, a bit of soil, a wheelbarrow.
He's a tall giraffe, a white puffy cloud.
Ace of spades, king of hearts, a laugh every minute.
He's as red as fire with the cue, banging a ball in every view.
He's a big blue tractor, it's in his blood.
He would help whoever he could
And you'll never stop my grandad.

James Hardy (13)
Queen Elizabeth's High School

WAR

Loss of life, what a waste,
Destruction of cities, a big disgrace.
Soldiers fighting side by side,
Their great fear, trying to hide.

The sky above darkened by plane after plane,
Dropping bombs which fall like rain.
Loud explosions fill the air,
People shouting and crying in despair.

Homeless families, herded in camps,
Having to live the life of tramps.
Hunger and dysentery the killer disease,
Spread through the camp with great ease.

Gone are the countries and their borders,
Welcome to the new world order.

Robert Baxter (12)
Queen Elizabeth's High School

I'M

I'm the bright blue sky and the Caribbean seas.
I'm a rough rock on a ragged mountainside.
I'm a hot spicy curry sizzling in your mouth.
I'm a big scary lion roaring in your ear.
I'm a stroke of lightning striking the moon.
I'm a football speeding into the back of the net.
I'm the smell of the salty sea blowing in the air.
I'm the roar of a tiger about to kill its prey.
I'm a great big, fast motorbike zooming rapidly down the road.
I'm a big sharp knife cutting some rope.

Thomas Aukland (12)
Queen Elizabeth's High School

MANHUNT

I ran to the fence
and laid low behind it,
watching my chasers go by.

My heart beat so loud,
I swear they could hear it,
but still they did not spot me.

I would have to make my move,
so I got into position
and jumped our from behind the fence.

I ran so fast,
as my legs could carry me,
to get to home base in a flash.

I managed to get
to the base,
without getting caught or trapped.

Knowing I had won,
I gave a sigh of relief,
and one awfully great cheer!

Nigel Linton (13)
Queen Elizabeth's High School

THE SURFER

The surfer reboards,
Elegant and graceful.
Kneeling, then crouching,
Rising and standing.

Knees slightly bent
And arms thrust outward,
The surfer's balance
Was smooth and assured.

The skill of the surfer
Was faultless, precise,
Perfect and flawless
And more dignified.

The rides were effortless,
Expertly done.
A fantastic display
And all done for fun.

Rebecca Lathrope (14)
Queen Elizabeth's High School

UTOPIA

Glinting,
It flickers,
Dancing shine in the sunlight stream.
Shafts of light caress the rock,
Striking the gold,
Smothered by the sand,
But through the spaces it glows,
Breaking into sparkle.

Lapping the shore,
The water surges, spraying surf,
Spitting the sand outwards,
Uncovering the flashes of gold,
Creating cascades of diamonds.
Rainbows shine through the water.
A pool of liquid silver trickles,
Back over the gold.
Diamonds lying,
Waiting to be found,
Unknown treasures sleep.

Katie Blower (16)
Queen Elizabeth's High School

VERTICAL

Looking up there's nothing there,
But bare rock, cold and wet,
Fingers bleeding, not daring to look down,
Upon the endless abyss below.

Adrenaline burning fierce and wild,
Determination strong and steadfast,
Fear is only a background colour,
Hope that luck is on your side.

Hands wedged in cracks,
Feet searching for a ledge,
Mind spinning with exhaustion,
Spurring the body to where it will not go,

Then it starts to get hard,
It's now or never,
Feet high near your arms,
Eyes closed, locked in effort.

Fingertip holds keep you there,
Suspended on the rock,
Then your fingers start to slip,
The slip tips the scales.

The fall is not the worst,
Hanging, waiting in a harness isn't a pleasant thing,
It bites like a lion if you stay too long,
Then determination returns.

What more could you ask for?
It's a lovely day and you've been pushed to your limits,
These are the joys of climbing.

Adam Looker (13)
Queen Elizabeth's High School

A TYPICAL SCHOOL DAY

Dead on seven my alarm rings
I crawl out of bed and get my things
I slowly go downstairs
Pour my breakfast and pull out one of the chairs
When my bowl is empty
I've got those stairs to climb, all twenty
Teeth cleaned and I'm washed and dressed,
I run downstairs and out the door, is it closed?

I run to the bus stop, I must dash
I've got a bus to catch
I do catch the bus in time
On the way the bus slows down on an uphill climb
There it is just ahead
That awful sickening dread

I'm off the bus, got to get to registration
Or I'll probably get an isolation
It's assembly next, that's usually boring
Then double history, someone will end up snoring
In history we're learning the causes of wars
And in geography we are learning contours.

In technology I wonder what we'll make
Then we've got a relaxing lunch break
In biology we dissect a heart
And in maths we are doing a chart
We've got French verbs to learn
And Bunsens in chemistry on the burn.

No more burning smell
There goes the bell
But now I've got a bus to get to
And when I get home, lots of homework to do.

James Watkins (13)
Queen Elizabeth's High School

THE POEM CURSER

I went to poem camp, I was the poet champ.
But now I cannot stop my rhyme,
Though I have tried time and time.
I rhyme in the morn, and in the eve,
I wish that this poetic curse would leave.
How can I get the beat out of my chat,
Leave it behind on another writer's doormat?
I suppose that I shall have to live with this cursed tongue,
Though I know that it won't be much fun,
Too much rhyming I shall lose all my friends!
And then, that's it, my social life ends.
I know, because whenever I talk, I rhyme,
From this day forward I am going to mime.
Instead of being the poets' champ,
I am packing my bags for mime camp!

Stephanie Winterbottom (12)
Queen Elizabeth's High School

GRANDMA DYING

My grandma loved me,
Even though she couldn't remember my name.
She'd try to speak to me
But she wouldn't be able to get the words out.
She would try and smile at me,
But her lips were so fragile that they hurt her.

She tried to explain about her homeland,
But she would get halfway through and forget what to say.
She would try to listen to us
But she would stop hearing halfway through.
Grandma would try to show us some photos
But just to get out of bed was a complete struggle.

I know my grandma loved me,
Even though she couldn't communicate,
All she ever wanted was for us, her family
To sit by her side forever more . . .

Eilidh Vizard (13)
Queen Elizabeth's High School

UNTITLED

Can you imagine . . .
Darren Gough saving a penalty?
Jimmy White in the middle of a scrum?
Tony Hawk shouting 'four'?

Michael Jordan bowling a yorkie?
Eric Bristow serving in deuce?
Emma Anderson hitting the back board?
Michael Owen smashing the puck?

Tiger Woods scoring a touchdown?
The Rock pulling off a grind?
Jerry Rice getting out of a snooker?
Will Carling potting the '8' ball.

Tim Henman catching a 8lb trout?
Wayne Gretzy scoring '180'?
Steve Davis pulling off a full nelson?
John Wilson swerving the red and blue flags?

All on live TV
Now that would be bizarre!

James Blakey (13)
Queen Elizabeth's High School

Rise

Eyes open, I'm not quite awake,
or aware of the natural beauty that surrounds me.
I yawn, slowly I stretch;
I shield my eyes from the bright, shimmering sun,
Its rays shining down from the clear sky up above.
I tune into birds, chirping sweetly their early morning tunes,
their songs so sweet to the ear,
like a little bit of heaven, in the form of beautiful music.
I recollect my thoughts,
my targets and aims for the long day ahead of me.
There is so much potential, I feel that anything is possible,
that I could achieve anything!
And then . . . I sink back into the luxurious comfort
of my warm, soft pillow.
The world, as they say, at my fingertips . . .

Mariam Omokanye (14)
Queen Elizabeth's High School

Money

I'll do anything for money,
Because money is my love.
I need that sweet bread and honey,
It's what I have to get hold of.
It comes straight out of the bank, into my purse,
One thing's for sure
I always get my money's worth.

Grace Lagzdins (13)
Queen Elizabeth's High School

DRAGON

It strides across the sandy floor,
leaving craters behind.
Tropical birds flutter away, terrified.
His breath is of fire, his claws are sharp;
his spiky tail whips around.
Thrashing palm trees down.
People stop.
People stare, again terrified.
He walks on, scaly skin
jagged back, eyes of evil.
Mind of a devil!

Sophie Cooke (13)
Queen Elizabeth's High School

I AM

I am a solid green blue.
I am a bright lamp.
I am a furry, brown beaver.
I am a loud, black electric guitar!
I am a ripe, red, healthy apple.
I am a fast, speedy Formula 1 car.
I am a chewy, chocolatey Mars bar.
I am a gold, shiny coin.
I am a warm paradise island.
I am a big, bulky encyclopaedia.

Oliver Joseph Ridgill (13)
Queen Elizabeth's High School

THE BEACH

The sea breeze blew through the swinging trees.
Which made you tingle and shake at the knees.
The copper coloured sand dunes and bright blue sea
Provided an atmosphere, so wonderful and free.
The leaning cottages and little old tea shops,
Crowded the alleyways that lead to the docks.
Tired fishermen sat with their nets,
Crouching over crab pots (their kind of pets)
Back on the beach with the golden sand,
The platform stands where once there was a band,
But no more is there life or the joyous grace,
Of this little beach, a now lonely place.

Eleanor Pilsworth (13)
Queen Elizabeth's High School

A POEM

My thoughts were calm and tranquil in the darkness.
The silence broke only by a kind of tapping.
Slowly the tapping turned to rattling,
Here comes the rain, slithering down the panes.
The window looks like a sheet of bubble wrap.
Now it has little rivulets running south.
A warm orange glow appears outside,
Was it some strange UFO?
No, it was time to close the curtains
And shut the glare of the street lights out.

Kelly Tate (17)
Queen Elizabeth's High School

ISOLATED FAITH

Inside, I cower
Torn, suffocated
Within the enclosing sphere of
Repulsive arrogance. An arrogance
Only glorified
By the superficial eyes of the world
Only hidden
By the beautiful flesh it lives within.
Since the vibrantly stained
Shards that compose
Your face
Pierce my heart alone.

'Insanity! Indoctrination!'
They cry,
With every fierce rip of my soul.
Or, deadly ignorance on their part?
My faithful passion
Coaxes me to challenge
The malicious doubt that
Creeps in
When I do not hear or feel
You.

Inside, I may cower
But the ultimate, eternal goal
I still strive to reach
Because in my heart
I know
I shall not cower forever.

Jennie Cottle (16)
Queen Elizabeth's High School

TRESPASSING THE AMAZING ME

I am the orangy yellow sun, shining down on the restless life.
I am the rough blue seas cascading against the tall rocks.
I am sweet dark chocolate inside a cake, round and warm.
I am the whispering wind floating through the harsh, barren desert.
I am the bright spark in the distance mesmerising the passers by.
I am a slithering snake winding round a lifeless tree stump.
I am the sour lemon juice on a sweet banoffee pie.
I am a swinging soft chimp leaping through the air of the dense
Amazon jungle.
I am a firey arrow sailing over a new battlefield ready to make my kill.
I am a sniffing puppy as it ventures out into new unknown land.

Dean Fishcher (12)
Queen Elizabeth's High School

ICH UBER MICH

I am a wet shade of royal blue with a dash of gold dust.
I am a rich odour of dark chocolate, a hint of silky caramel.
I am a strong curry with a pinch of sugar.
I am a heavy metal with solid chords.
I am a colourful rainbow with a pot of gold at my feet.
I am a round pebble waiting to be thrown into the vast sea.
I am a fiery dragon breathing powerful fumes.
I am a shiny new mountain bike whizzing down the hill.
I am a single page stranded on this huge web.

Fred Ashbolt (11)
Queen Elizabeth's High School

MY HEAD'S IN A JAM

My head's in a jam
can't take you off my mind
from the time we met
I've been beset
by thoughts of you
and the more that I ignore these feelings
the more I find myself believing
that I just have to see you again.

I can't let you pass me by
I just can't let you go
but I know that I am much
too shy to let you know
afraid that I might say
the wrong word and displease you
afraid for love to fade
before it can come true
like a child again
I'm at a loss for words
how does one define a crush combined with longing
longing to possess you oh so dearly
I'm obsessed by you completely
I'll go mad
if I can't have you

I can't let you pass me by
I just can't let you go
let me say the things
say the words and let you know
I would rather say the awkward words than lose you
or for love to fade before it can come true.

Jonathan Spurr (13)
St Mary's Catholic High School, Grimsby

THE DEMON DRAGON SLAYER

The demon dragon dragged his prey
Back to his lair
And with one puff from
His mighty breath
He fried his prey and gulped
Him down in one.

Snap!
He hears a twig snap outside
And turns like a whistle
And like a rocket he races outside
Flying up into the air
He lands on the ground
With a loud thundering
Bang!

The fight began
Fire here, fire there, fire everywhere
But the brave young knight
Throws his sword like a grenade
And hits his target
On his finned wing
The dragon wails in pain
And drops down dead!

J G Kavanagh (14)
St Mary's Catholic High School, Grimsby

MISSING YOU

I hear you in the wind when I'm walking down the street
I think you're there on a summer's day and my life is so complete.
It seems like only yesterday since you slipped away and sometimes
I wish you would knock on the door and simply say 'Hey'.
You need to be here in each and every way to be our dad,
husband and friend.
Going so soon and so young, thinking it was just a dream,
And you would come back in the end,
But knowing you are gone it is so hard to live on
We all love you and I know that you walk with us,
In our hearts every day.

Charlie Gray (13)
St Mary's Catholic High School, Grimsby

PEOPLE AROUND US

Things around the world today
Laughter, crying, people pray.
People who die from unclean water
Animals that die, cows, pigs, sheep slaughter.
We think that money or gold means much more
But what would be important to the poor.
A golden ring, a glass of drink
Which one of these do you think?
We would choose the golden ring
We would be happy and dance and sing
Just to feel the touch on an old man's finger
The waiting's far too long
They will not linger.

Rebecca Cliffe (12)
Skegness Grammar School

THE TINY FAIRY

I've found a tiny fairy in the treasure chest
Think it must have come from the attic
Because it's dusty and smells all fusty
And its wings are broken.

I fed it on many things, tried bread,
The icing off cake, bananas and chocolate,
But it stared at me as if to say,
I don't want food, I want to play.

It made a mess among the house
Not unlike a baboon but smaller
It is out of place here
And it is quite mournful.

If you believed in it I would come
Straight away to your door to let you share my wonder
But I want instead to see
If you yourself will pass this way.

Lauren Lake (12)
Skegness Grammar School

A BABY KOALA

I've found a baby koala in my tree.
Think it must have come from far,
maybe Australia, because it's warm
and cute and its feet are in the air.

I fed it on many things, tried leaves,
the skin of banana, soup and coffee.
But it stared up at me as if to say,
I can't eat those things, I'm only small.

It made a perch among my bedposts,
not unlike a bird's, but without leaves
and moss, it's quite out of place here
and is quite sleepy.

If you believed in it I would say,
hurry to my house to let you share my wonder,
but I want instead to see
if you yourself will pass this way.

Jenny Green (12)
Skegness Grammar School

A SQUEAKING MOUSE

I found a squeaking mouse in my bedsitter
I think it must've come from the depths of the basement
because its mouth and eyes and fur
are flecked browny-black.

I fed it on many things, tried cheese,
the crusts of bread, milk and wood
but it stared up at me as if to say,
you can't help me, I find my own food.

It made a house below my bed
not unlike a mouse's hole
but it is made in my mattress.
It is out of place here and is quite shrill.

If you believed in it I would come
to your cellar to let you share my wonder
but I want instead to see
if you yourself will pass this way.

Lauren Reavy (12)
Skegness Grammar School

VALENTINE

Not a red rose or a satin heart.

I give you a pencil.
It is the truth enveloped with gloss.
It promises secrecy,
like the forgotten past of a lover.

Here.
It will blunt when you most need it,
like a lover.
It will frustrate you and torment you,
like a lover.

I am trying to be truthful.

Not a cute card or a kissogram.

I give you a pencil.
Create words with it.
Recall memories with it.
Until the pencil is sharpened away
as our love is.

Take it.
It represents eternity,
if you like.
Lethal.
Its words cling to your memory.
Cling to you, for life.

Alix Gribby (16)
Skegness Grammar School

VALENTINE

Not a red rose or a satin heart,

I give you a lipstick,
A blood-red facade forging the truth,
Creating deceptive beauty,
Like the powerful blinding of love.

Here,
Giving an improved effigy of belief,
A mask to remove anxiety
To remain pure in your lover's eyes,
Misrepresented

I am trying to be truthful,

Not a cute card or a kissogram,

I give you a lipstick,
It will reveal actions of infidelity
With a lover in a moment of intensity,
Passionate, heaving,
As we are,
For as long as we are.

Take it,
It will implode feelings of guilt,
If you like,
Its murderous grasp clinging to your lips
Like a kiss, diminishing . . .

Jodie Waterhouse (16)
Skegness Grammar School

VALENTINE

Not a red rose or a satin heart.

I give you a seed.
It is small and feeble.
It grows and expands
Like the beautiful flourishing of love.

Here.
It will exist only to grow and prosper
It is shining.
Beautiful at its peak
Like eternal love, unending, everlasting.

I am trying to be truthful.

Not a cute card or kissogram.

I give you a seed.
Its existence is only minor, its progression slow.
Unknown and undying
Like our love
For as long as our love is.

Take it,
Its importance seems insignificant,
But watch it.
Amazing.
Its strength will overwhelm you,
Stay with you.

Hayley Richard-Jones (15)
Skegness Grammar School

VALENTINE

Not a red rose or a satin heart.

I give you a key.
It has the power to change you.
It will provoke your curiosity
Like the start of a new romance.

Here.
Take it and use it as you will,
To open up a whole new world,
Or to hide your feelings
And lock yourself away.

I am trying to be truthful.

Not a cute card or a kissogram.

I give you a key.
That can open new ways,
To happiness and love.
Wear it to feel as secure
As you can, like being with me.

Take it.
For until you use it,
You will not know if it is the key
To my heart.

Kristina Miller (15)
Skegness Grammar School

VALENTINE

Not a red rose or a satin heart.

I give you an ink cartridge.
It is a capsule of emotions filled to the brim.
At first it is strong,
full, like the passionate beginning of love.

Here.
Let your deepest feelings open up,
circulate and pour.
It is the key to honesty and when in its home
you can express yourself.

I am trying to be truthful.

Not a cute card or kissogram.

I give you an ink cartridge.
It gradually becomes weaker, like emptying emotions,
purposeless and concluding
as we are.
It has nearly disappeared.

Take it.
It represents our love, diminishing but remaining
if you like.
Vacant.
The blue liquid pours like tears over the waste, the memories.
Then forgotten.

Hayley Mould (15)
Skegness Grammar School

VALENTINE

Not a red rose or a satin heart.

I give you a jigsaw.
It is placed in a cardboard box.
It promises the full picture,
piece by piece
like the steady progression of a relationship.

Here.
It will need you to have patience,
like a lover.
It will make you apprehensive,
as you consider what it's worth.

I am trying to be truthful.

Not a cute card or a kissogram.

I give you a jigsaw.
Its many pieces will entice you.
Dedicated or infatuated?
As we are,
for as long as we are.

Take it.
When you finish; you can keep it
if you like.
Addictive.
A piece is mislaid; a part is vacant
like an empty heart.
Pointless; time lost forever.

Jessica Cummings (16)
Skegness Grammar School

VALENTINE

Not a red rose or a satin heart.

I give you a watch.
The sparkling serenity of time
captured upon your wrist
like the infinite hours of our love.

Here.
The hypnotic tick-tock, tick
enchants and enthrals
with its sweet serenading
like a lover.

I'm trying to be truthful.

Not a cute card or a kissogram.

I give you a watch.
Its metallic shimmering, dances like a firefly;
energetic and sensual.
As we are.
For as long as we are.

Take it.
Its platinum link, encircle your wrist, like a close embrace
if you like.
Choking.
The cold steel strangles your bare skin;
entombing and everlasting.

Tim Jackson (15)
Skegness Grammar School

VALENTINE

Not a red rose or a satin heart.

I give you a letter.
It is my feelings all written down on paper.
It promises love
Like the tender touch of a kiss.

Here.
It will fill your head with confusion
Like a lover
It will make your thoughts
A chaotic spiral of perplexity.

I am trying to be truthful.

Not a cute card or a kissogram.

I give you a letter.
Its sharp paper edges may cut your hands,
Biting and painful
As love is,
For as long as love lasts

Take it.
Its meaningless words merge into a love poem
If you like.
Lethal.
Its words will linger in your mind,
Consume your being.

Lynsey Reeves (15)
Skegness Grammar School

IRONWOOD

Those two choppers were so busy
Slicing into the root
The chips danced
Thin, little blocks came away
From the old monster.

The man and the axe seemed to be partners
Swift, powerful strokes
The axe sweeping under the tremendous tower of strength
Chewing into the roots with bites.

Together the men heaved against the stump,
Pressure,
They tackled the old stump,
The chips danced
Dirt was coming from between the cut roots.

They tackled too another root,
Striking the wood,
In a steady rhythm of double blows,
They stood in silence,
As they sliced into the last root.

Toni Browne (11)
Skegness Grammar School

A BABY ELEPHANT

I've found a baby elephant in the garden shed,
Think it must have come from the circus down the road,
Because it's small and grey and its ears are big and hairy
Like fat balloons at a circus fair.

I fed it on many things, tried oats, the cream of milk,
Carrots and cabbages, but it stared at me as if to say;
I'm a poor baby elephant and I've lost my way.

It made a doo-doo among the tools,
Not unlike a dog's but bigger.
It is out of place here and is quite unhappy.

If you believed in it I would arrive on your doorstep
To let you share my wonder, but I want instead to see,
If you yourself will pass this way.

Jeanette Cawley (12)
Skegness Grammar School

IRONWOOD

Father halted
Humped shoulders
Drew a deep breath
Wrapped his big hands
The fingers curled
Concentrated cold fire
Surge of power
He heaved
Tossed his axe
Breathing hard
Strike
Swift powerful strokes
Glow of the sun
Silence
Slid his shoulders down the stump
Inch by inch
Surge of power
Mass
Rocked forward
Dirt tearing loose
Ease
Ancient foundation.

Victoria Coleman (11)
Skegness Grammar School

VALENTINE

Not a red rose or a satin heart.

I give you a mirror.
To reflect upon our time
To remember the days as we were
To reveal the hidden
To reveal the truth.

Look.
Let it illuminate your heart.
Intense, vivid, brilliant
Touched simply by the eye.

I am trying to be truthful.

Not a cute card or a kissogram.

I give you a mirror.
On the outside admiration
On the inside judgement
See what you want to see
Reflections do not have to be real.

Look deeper.
What do you really see?
Your mind distorts your heart
Honesty.
All you see
A hologram.

Emily Kindness (15)
Skegness Grammar School

IRONWOOD

He stood in silence
Cold, concentrated fire
Evoked -
Danger within.

Great arc, sweeping . . .
Steel biting into wood
Chewing, chewing
Chips dance in terror -
Dirt tears loose.

Whirling . . .
Stroke
Clear ringing sound . . .
Slicing . . . wrestling with the old monster
An old friend.
Uncut root 'slice'
Last strip . . . blade sank.

They are one
Partners
Old master . . . battling.

Ancient foundations
Tearing loose.
Sucking sound
A grotesque new angle
Smash

A tremendous tower of strength
Sprawled.
Sprawled in the dirt.
Manpower.

Daniel Wilkinson (11)
Skegness Grammar School

THE HOLIDAY

I went on holiday last year
My baby brother was sick in the air
As soon as we landed he said he was hungry
He started to whine again!

We got to the hotel
And went for a swim
Until my baby brother said it was dim
Oh, stop complaining my mum said
He started to whine again!

We went out for dinner
To a very nice restaurant
And he pulled off the tablecloth
Mum had a go at him for being so naughty
He started to whine again!

The holiday was over
We were going back home
My brother was fine, until
Oh not again!

David Newman (11)
Skegness Grammar School

A MASSIVE CAT

I've found a massive cat in the volcano.
Think it must have come from high up at Mars.
Because it's green and brisky and pink!
Spots are still reflecting in its eyes.

I fed it on many things, tried dirt,
The cheese from my fridge, nuts and haggis,
But it stared up at me as if to say,
Who are you? take me to my own home.

It made a bed among the quilt,
Not unlike a human's but larger, it
Is out of place here and it is,
Quite funny.

If you believed in it I would rush,
To your house as fast as I could,
To you and let you share my fantasy,
But I want instead to see if you yourself
Will pass this way.

Jason Butler (12)
Skegness Grammar School

A TALKING LION

I've found a talking lion in the garden,
Think he must come from the circus,
Because he's dressed up and tired and clowns
Are still reflecting in his eyes.

I fed him on many things, tried pig,
The leg of a man, milk and beef
But he looked up at me and he said,
'I need a place to hide.'

He made a shelter among the sofa,
Unlike a tent but weaker,
He is out of his place here,
And is quite silent.

If you believed, I would come,
And show you this strange creature
To let you share my wonder,
But I want instead to see
If you yourself will pass this way.

Thomas Baron (12)
Skegness Grammar School

SHANE POEM

Father halted, legs wide, hands on hips,
Steady rhythm,
Slicing the wood as the chips dance.
Tremendous tower of strength,
Hidden hardness,
They pound smoothly into each stroke,
Desperate in determination,
Old monster,
Blade sank in once more
Slow dogged pace
Parallel groves
Big double bladed axe
Striking the wood
Releasing the pressure as they heave
Sweat pouring
Swift powerful strokes,
Muscles locked in that great sustained effort
Heaving, blowing, tearing, clenching,
They brought the dirt out between the cut roots,
The axe was set head, on the ground.

Emma Rawlins (12)
Skegness Grammar School

IRONWOOD

Working steadily away
Swinging the axe,
Making the chips dance,
Slicing the tough old wood,
Together they heaved against the stump,
The blade sank in once more,
Chewing into the root,
The stump quivered,
Swift powerful hitting tough old wood
Making the chips dance.

That old monster,
Uncut root,
Steel biting into wood,
Steady rhythm of double blows
Hitting a fast pace,
That old monster!

Lauren Chantry (11)
Skegness Grammar School

IRONWOOD

He stood in silence,
A tremendous tower of strength,
Striking the wood,
At a slow dogged pace,
Chewing into the roots of
The ancient foundation,
The chips danced.

Swift, powerful strokes,
Slicing into the root,
Heaved,
Tackled,
Battled with it,
Steady rhythm of double blows,
Finishing it with manpower.

The old stump,
An old monster,
With hidden hardness,
Smashed,
Into a grotesque new angle,
Standing in silence.

Richard Glenn (11)
Skegness Grammar School

IRONWOOD

Big old stump, blade sank
Chopping, slicing, chips dance
Squared, straightened, wrestled, smash
A massive blow of a swinging axe
A big steady rhythm of double blows
An ancient foundation of powerful strokes
A straightened blade through ironwood
With a gnawing sharp powerful thud
The root was cut, an axe swung
A strange pattern against the glow of the sun.
Pulsing in one incredible surge of power
An axe on the stump slicing deeper and deeper
Big old stump like an old friend
Silence was complete, it was the end.

Carolyn Sparkes (11)
Skegness Grammar School

IRONWOOD

Manpower
Smash
partners
Swift powerful strokes
Chewing into the roots
Chips dance
Hidden hardness

Battling
Show dogged pace
Clear ringing sound
Ancient foundation
Swinging a great arc,
Poured
Sliced
Bringing out the uncut roots.

Sucking sound
Swing back biting his roots
Bringing the dirt out
Poured
Willed
Battling
Hidden hardness.

Josh Whittam (11)
Skegness Grammar School

My Family

Early morning when I woke up, I went to my mum's bed,
I shouted in her earhole, 'Mum are you dead!'
I thought my mum might not give a reply,
But being she, she wasn't shy,
On her table she fiercely tapped,
And I got harshly slapped.

Then I went downstairs to Dad,
And he looked extremely mad,
As soon as he caught a glimpse of me,
He shouted, 'Ben, pour me a cup of tea.'
I couldn't really refuse to do so,
Unless I wanted to leave and go.

I thought my little brother would like
Some company, so I gave him a try,
He was in his bedroom watching TV,
He got off his bed said, 'Hello,' and punched me!
This was my last straw,
I couldn't take it anymore.

I ran downstairs and out the door,
And I never go back anymore.

Ben Hardy (11)
Skegness Grammar School

THE CAT

There is a cat as black as midnight
Who I see walking along the street
Moving along the road elegantly
Watching out for people's feet.

She sees a dog running along the road
So she hides and he goes on
She carries on walking like the brave cat she is
But I think she's glad he's gone.

It's getting late
And soon it's deep into the night
Strolling along
Her eyes shining bright.

She can't wait to get home
And go through the cat door
Have her night meal
And curl up on the floor.

These thoughts carry her away
And soon she's actually there
Running inside
And jumping on the chair.

Kristen Ballantyne (11)
Skegness Grammar School

A HUGE ELEPHANT

I've found a huge elephant in the wild,
Think it must have come from one of those safari parks in Africa,
Because it's dirty and mouldy and has mud splodges all over it.

I fed it on many things, tried grass, coconuts from two years ago,
Bananas and seeds but it stared up at me as if to say;
Leave me alone and take me back home.

It made a house among the rubble in the corner
Not unlike a human's but dirtier, it is out of place here
And is quite a mess.

If you believed in it I would run as fast as I could
To your house and show you my world,
But I want instead to see if you yourself will pass this way.

Liam Dabbs (12)
Skegness Grammar School

IRONWOOD

Old stump,
Ancient foundation,
Uncut roots.

One incredible surge,
Swinging the axe,
Whirled, smashed,
The chips danced.

Clear ringing sound,
Steady rhythm of double blows,
Bringing the dirt out.

Concentrated cold fire,
Little sucking sound,
Swift powerful strokes,
Steel biting into wood.

Uncut root,
Parallel grooves,
Those two choppers,
Tackled another root,
Finish it with manpower.

Alice Brooks (11)
Skegness Grammar School

Ironwood

Steel biting into wood
Slicing into wood
Smashed!
Striking the wood
Blade sank
Deep as father could drive
Battling
Big old stump
Steady rhythm
Chips danced
Last strip
Released the pressure
Parallel grooves
Big old stump
Old master
Released the pressure
Ancient foundation.

Nevada Wood (11)
Skegness Grammar School

Ironwood

He stood in silence
He poked his axe into the opening and I heard it strike wood,
That old stump
Tremendous tower of strength
The blade would sink into the parallel grooves,

Steady rhythm of double blows
They were making the chips dance
The dirt was tearing loose all around it
The blade sank in once more
Swinging the axe in steady rhythm.

Swift powerful blows
Ancient foundation
The axe sliced through the last strip and the root was cut
Old monster
Tackled.

Cathryn Smith (11)
Skegness Grammar School

A WHITE UNICORN

I've found a white unicorn
near my house
think it must have come from the
forbidden forest,
because it's wet and dirty,
trees are still flashing,
in its star-like eyes.

I fed it on many things,
tried cakes, roots of trees, leaves,
and sandwiches.
But it stared up at me as if to say,
I don't think so, man!

It made a patch among the leaves,
not unlike a mouse's,
but larger.
It is out of place here,
and is quite depressed.

If you believed,
I would show you it,
and come to let you share my wonder,
but I want instead to see,
if you yourself will pass this way.

Sophie Bowler (12)
Skegness Grammar School

IRONWOOD

A clear ringing sound
of steel biting into wood
deep breaths
old stump
old friend

Double blows
digging into the tough wood
old stump
old friend

The foundation crumbled
the chips danced
old stump
old friend

Swift powerful strokes
soared through the air
old stump
old friend.

Tony Howitt (11)
Skegness Grammar School

IRONWOOD

He stood in silence,
Hitting a fast pace making the chips dance,
The blade would sink into the parallel grooves,
Grunting, arguing, battling.

Striking, smashing, slicing,
The uncut roots,
Steady rhythm of double blows,
Serene and contented.

Concentrated cold fire,
Whirling the axe,
Soft sucking sound,
Fierce energy,
Incredible strength,
Finishing it with manpower,
He stood in silence.

Nina Harrison (11)
Skegness Grammar School

HAMSTER

Hamster runs in his wheel
In and out of his tubes
He nags on his cage bars
And searches for food.

When hamster is asleep
He's silent as a rock
But when he's wide awake
He's noisier than us lot.

When I let him out of his cage
He runs round and round in circles
Take your eyes off him for a second
And he shoots off behind the sofa.

Pick him up in your hand
Hold him there and he will wash
Put him back in his cage,
And he will run off to his bed.

Kurtis Kennedy (11)
Skegness Grammar School

A Tiny Goblin

I've found a tiny goblin in the garden.
Think it must have come from a far away planet
Because it's strange and foreign
And its skin is a fluorescent yellow.

I fed it on many things, tried chips,
The scraps of dinner, meat and vegetables
But it stared up at me as if to say,
We don't eat this on our planet.

It made a home among the bushes
Not unlike a cat's but smaller,
It is out of place here
And is quite sad.

If you believed in it I would invite you
Round to my house to let you share my wonder,
But I want instead to see
If you yourself will pass this way.

Melanie Priestley (12)
Skegness Grammar School

Ironwood

He stood in silence,
muscles locked,
steady rhythm of double blows,
striking the wood,
out the chips danced,
smashed,
steel biting wood,
smashed, great arc in the root,
tremendous tower of strength,
hidden hardness, battling,
old monster, battling,
old stump, tackling.

Sweat rivulets, bringing the dirt,
axe head, smashed, slow dogged pace,
whirled, swung back to his root,
parallel grooves, ancient foundation,
little sucking sound, mighty streaked,
uncut root, he stood in silence,
steady rhythm of double blows,
striking the wood, battling,
smashed, smashed, smashed,
discernible movement, muscles locked,
he stood in silence.

Joshua Lindley (11)
Skegness Grammar School

AN OLD DWARF

I've found an old dwarf in the bushes.
Think it must have come from the old cottage over the field
because its cosy and calm and warm feeling
is still reflecting in its eyes.

I fed it on many things, tried potato,
the inside of walnuts, carrots and apples,
but it stared up at me as if to say,
I don't like these foods you offer me.

It made a bed among the washing,
not unlike a person's but smaller,
it is out of place here
and is quite weary.

If you believed in it I would sprint
to your house as fast as I could to let you share my wonder
but I want instead to see if you yourself will pass this way.

Emilio Paiva De Brito (12)
Skegness Grammar School

IRONWOOD

Curious dogged pace,
Fingers curled,
Large fists,
Steady rhythm of double blows,
Monster.

Tremendous tower of strength,
Clean shaven,
Hidden hardness,
The chips danced
Swift powerful strokes,
Monster.

Without slackening pace,
Parallel grooves,
Swinging the axe,
Steel biting wood,
Monster.

Almost as deep as it could drive,
Old stump,
Swung,
Splendid in the battle,
Monster.

Humped shoulders,
Striking wood,
Frowned upon faces,
Old monster,
Monster.

Lyndsay Bell (11)
Skegness Grammar School

NIGHT-TIME

Bang!
I jumped out of bed.
What was that?
I turned my head,
There was a face staring right at me!
Oh, it's just my dressing gown.

I walked over to the window,
It must have been that which had woken me,
I could hear the wails of the wind,
Like ghosts screaming.

The swing was rocking back and forth,
As if someone was on it with nothing to do,
Perhaps a ghostly figure,
Invisible.

I walked outside looking around,
A claw crept up behind me,
I ran to get away from it,
Just the branch of that big tree.

I turned the corner,
Two bright eyes blinded me,
Continuously staring at me,
Walking closer Mum had left the car lights on.

The wind again telling me to go,
I tiptoed back up to my room,
Jumped into my sheets,
And in a blink there was daylight.

Freddie Dowker (11)
Skegness Grammar School

IRONWOOD

Steel biting into wood
Striking the wood,
Uncut root
Steady rhythm of double blows
Old stump
Sudden chill
Hidden hardness.

Swinging
Chopping
Hitting
Striking
Parallel grooves,
Smashing
Bashing
Tackling
Battling.

Clear ringing sound.
Old stump.
Chop!
Strike!
Uncut root - cut root!

Camilla Barker (11)
Skegness Grammar School

MUMS AND DADS

You probably see your mum as
Bossy, fussy and always nagging
And you probably see your dad as
Embarrassing, old and always complaining.

But you probably don't see that they're so much more,
They're special, caring and maybe sometimes a bore.

Who was always there when you came home from school
And needed a cuddle?
Or who was there when children laughed and made fun
When you fell in a puddle?

You do not realise how wonderful they are,
Both with them and sometimes far.

Madeline Dyson (12)
Skegness Grammar School

THE NEW ARRIVAL

'Can I have a gerbil Mum?'
'You can't,' is what Mum said.
'I'm sorry love,' she added
'But I'm having a baby instead.'

'I'd rather have a gerbil, Mum,
With its eyes all gleaming and red
Than a little screaming baby
Who never lets me go to bed.'

'Please can I have a gerbil Mum?
I'll feed it everyday,
You won't have to do a thing Mum,
Except stay in bed and lay.'

'All right,' said Mum, 'you've won again,
I'll tell you what to do
If you help me with the baby
You have the gerbil too.'

I got the gerbil I wanted,
I help Mum everyday,
The baby isn't too bad,
But the gerbil's quieter I'd say!

Chantelle Stanbra (11)
Skegness Grammar School

IRONWOOD

Shane stood and looked,
Staring at the old monster.
He stood in silence,
Looking at the hidden hardness.

Then with a tremendous tower of strength he swung,
Swinging with mightiness at the parallel grooves,
Striking the wood as the chips danced in the air.

Swift powerful strokes slicing into the roots,
Tackling the stump,
A steady rhythm started to flow
As he took double blows,
Shane's pure strength was weakening the old monster.

With wood flying in all directions,
Then the wood fell to the ground
And silence fell.

Ashley Redgard (11)
Skegness Grammar School

A LOST KITTEN

I've found a fluffy kitten in the bush,
Think it must have come from a cattery,
Because it's clean and healthy
And her eyes are really small and sweet.

I fed it on many things, tried beef,
The gravy off pork, milk and chicken,
But it stared up at me as if to say
I'm a poor little kitten and I've lost my way.

It made a bed among my jumper,
Not unlike a cat's but smaller,
It is out of place here,
And is quite sad.

If you believed in it I would run
Along to your house to let you share my wonder,
But I want instead to see
If you yourself will pass this way.

Kate Dennis (12)
Skegness Grammar School

THE SCHOOL MONSTER

On the edge of the playground
Down the slippery stairs
Saw a monster with a long face
Covered in sweaty hairs.

He had a handful of jewellery
Stolen from little boys
He confiscated books and comics
And all their favourite toys.

He wore a sweaty jacket
Looked similar to The Undertaker
More gruesome than a horror film
He was the school caretaker.

He spoke a bit like my grandad
All very, very low
It sounds a bit like a motorbike
And says it very slow.

On the edge of the playground
Down the slippery stairs
Saw a monster with a long face
Covered in sweaty hairs.

Scott Worthington (11)
Skegness Grammar School

SLEEP, SLEEP, SLEEP

Outside there's a giant dog,
Walking the streets.
He gives a polite and courteous 'hello'
To everyone he meets,
As I sleep, sleep, sleep.

Tom Cruise is out there,
He's just shot someone!
I'm telling you he's a mass murderer,
Somebody catch that con.
As I snore, snore, snore.

My hall carpet has just turned red,
My hamster's all dressed up.
My nightie is all glittery and fancy,
Guess what, I've just won the dream cup!
This all happens as I sleep, snore, dream . . . dream.

Tiffany Clark (11)
Skegness Grammar School

A FLUFFY RABBIT

I've found a fluffy rabbit in the rose bush.
Think it must have come from the hairdressers
because it's got fluffy fur that smells like hairspray
and the hair clippings are still in its eyes.

I fed it on many things, tried pork,
bits of lamb and chocolate,
but it looked at me as if to say,
sorry, I'm a vegetarian.

It made a bed among the laundry,
not unlike a rabbit's but tidier,
it is out of place here
and is quite bossy.

If you believed it I would tell it to the world
to let you share my wonder,
but instead I want to see
if you yourself will pass this way.

Laura Richards (12)
Skegness Grammar School

THE CRAZY HOUSE

Early morning, late at night,
My bro' wakes up and gives me a fright.
His hair stuck up, standing on end,
Ever heard of a brush my friend?

Then at six, every morning,
You hear my little sister yawning.
Now she's coming down the stairs,
Clomp! Clomp! Clomp! The bang's in pairs.

Now it's Mum's turn to be loud,
Look at her clothes, nothing to be proud.
All pink and silky, white and red,
Why couldn't she have stayed in bed?

Dad, ready to scream and shout,
Bangs on the door and yells, 'Let me out!
This crazy house is driving me mad,
Oi! Get out of bed, you're just as bad!'

I jump up and brush my hair,
Ready for a normal day, ever been there?
I try and try to calm him down,
It never works, he's still the clown!

So now you know what it's like to be me,
I would never change it, well, maybe!

Laura Phipps (11)
Skegness Grammar School

PLEASE TAKE YOUR DOG OUT OF HERE

Please take that dog home
Before I lock it out?
I stroked it for hours
As it came wondering in, I had to shout,
I took its disgraceful collar
And took away its bone
But now he's asleep
I can eat my cone.

And don't think for a moment
That I wanted it here
Why he was wagging his tail
I was stood in fear
He broke my china doll
That I got when I was small
Would you mind getting me a new one?
I got it from the mall.

Of course I was angry
When I threw him down the stairs
He lay at the bottom whining
He was so scared
I'm sort of glad he wasn't hurt
He came running back up
He licked me to death
Before he smashed my brand new cup.

So please take him out of here
Before I lock him out.

Stacie McEwen (11)
Skegness Grammar School

WITCH'S BROTH

Slip slop goes our pot,
Lots of things in there to rot.

Devil's horn, baby's cry,
Deaf man's ear, blind man's eye.
Jupiter's spot, Saturn's ring,
Fox's bite and wasp sting.

Slip slop goes our pot,
Lots of things in there to rot.

Mouse's squeak, rat's tail,
Shark's jaw, song of whale.
Ghostly call, hyena laugh,
Dirty water from a bath.

Slip slop goes our pot,
Lots of things in there to rot.

Nail clippings, hair from a wig,
Mouldy cheese and a shrivelled up fig.
Old man's sock, a lion's lair,
No room in our pot left for us to spare.

Slip slop goes our pot,
Lots of things in there to rot.

Sophie Hardy (11)
Skegness Grammar School

The Wind Is My Best Friend

The wind blows the washing,
It curls me up in bed,
It drifts my dreams away
And shows me where to stay.

It helps the leaves fall off in autumn,
So the roads look pretty,
It drives over the woods on winter nights
And makes me shut my window tight.

It blows my homework away
And my teachers tell me off.
People hate the wind but I like him lots,
He is my best friend
And I talk to him lots.

Alice Bone (11)
Skegness Grammar School

I Miss

I miss the way he whistles when he fed all his cats,
I miss the way he cackled and always made me laugh,
I miss the way his hair stuck out on end,
I miss the sound of his crutches, click, clack, click, clack,
I miss him always laughing, his great toothless smile,
I miss hugging his bony chest,
I miss his moustache tickling my cheek,
I miss him crushing snails with his crutches and cooking
                              home-made chips and hot dogs,
But what I miss mostly is not being able to see him.

I miss my grandad.

Emma Easton (11)
Skegness Grammar School

LITTLE SISTERS

Little sisters, I have one of my own
In fact she's very noisy when I'm talking on the phone,
Terrible little thing, what should I do?
'Oi! I'm telling on you.'

'Leave me alone, I'm going out.'
'Can I come with you?' she starts to shout,
'You messy mite, have a nap
If you're good I'll bring you something back.'

'Stop crying, stop crying, please, please, please!
You're giving me a headache, I'll smack your knees,'
Yes! She's finally asleep,
Goodnight, goodnight Little Bo Peep.

Sally Checkley (11)
Skegness Grammar School

MY PRECIOUS BOX

I will put into my box the loving, warm-hearted feeling from
my family and friends.
I will put into my precious box the lip licking laces
of spaghetti Bolognese.
I will put into my precious box the likeness of my football gear.

I will not put into my precious box the homework
from school.
I will not put into my precious box the telling-off
from my dad.
I will not put into my precious box the frequent nagging
of my mum.
I will not put into my precious box the awful weather
from Scunthorpe.

Luke Page & Martin (11)
South Leys School

MY PRECIOUS BOX

I will put into my precious box
    the caring of my family.
I will also put into my precious box
    the good times I have with my friends.
I will also put into my precious box
    the mouth-watering taste of scrumptious food.
I will also put into my precious box
    the minty feeling of mint chocolate chip ice cream.
I will also put into my precious box
    the interactive fun of my Game Boy.

I will not put into my precious box
    the disgusting smell of bins.
I will also not put into my precious box
    the creepy crawly spiders.
I will also not put into my precious box
    the noisiness of annoying boys and girls.
I will also not put into my precious box
    the constant arguing of me and my sister.
I will also not put into my precious box
    the disgusting taste of disgusting food and drink.

Claire Gardner (11)
South Leys School

MY PRECIOUS BOX

I will put into my precious box the laughter and love and warmth
                          of my family.
I will put into my precious box the sound and rhythm of my stereo.
I will put into my precious box the care and laughter of my friends.
I will put into my precious box the joy and humour of my books.
I will put into my precious box the meltiness and stickiness
                         of chocolate.

I will put into my precious box the flashing lights of my computer.
I will put into my precious box the comfort of my clothes.
I will put into my precious box the historical element of my necklace.

I will not put into my precious box the creepiness of spiders.
I will not put into my precious box the taste of stuffing.

Amy Jones (11)
South Leys School

MY PRECIOUS BOX

I will put into my precious box the loving kindness personality
                                of my family.
I will put into my precious box the sentimental comfort of the
                                picture of my grandma.
I will put into my precious box the comfort of my teddy.
I will put into my precious box the excitement of money.
I will put into my precious box the satisfying taste of food.
I will put into my precious box the entertainment of television.
I will put into my precious box the stimulating sound of my music.
I will put into my precious box the excitement of shopping.
I will put into my precious box the safety of my mobile.
I will put into my precious box the hygienic neatness of my hairbrush.

I will not put into my precious box the chilling feeling of the
                                long hairy legs of spiders.
I will not put into my precious box the burning and the knotted
                                stomach feeling of embarrassment.
I will not put into my precious box the rush that goes through of fear.
I will not put into my precious box the sickening taste of tomatoes.
I will not put into my precious box the upsetting feeling of cruelty.

Kirsty Wood (11)
South Leys School

MY PRECIOUS BOX

I will put into my precious box the security and warmth of my family.
I will put into my precious box the helpful information of my mobile.
I will put into my precious box the laughter of my friends.
I will put into the precious box the comfiness of my bed.
I will put into my precious box the love and warmth of my cats.
I will put into my precious box the interactive fun of my PC.

I will not put into my precious box the horrible taste of
green vegetables.
I will not put into my precious box the annoyingness of my brother.
I will not put into my precious box the struggle of getting out
of bed in the morning.
I will not put into my precious box the annoying bleeping noise
of my alarm.
I will not put into my precious box the unhygienic smell of my bin.
I will not put into my precious box the formality of a Sunday dinner.

Ashley Drinkall (11)
South Leys School

MY PRECIOUS BOX

I will put in my precious box the adventures and suspense of
my Harry Potter books.
I will put in my precious box the happiness and laughter of my family.
I will put in my precious box the warmth and colours of my clothes.
I will put in my precious box the softness of my teddy.
I will put in my precious box the warmth and softness of my bed.

I will not put in my precious box the smell and the flies in my bin.
I will not put in my precious box the big-headedness of boys.
I will not put in my precious box the fights between family members.

Kirsty Hare (11)
South Leys School

My Precious Box

I will put into my precious box the love and security of
          my happy family.
I will put into my precious box the brilliant flavour and
          sweet taste of my food.
I will put into my precious box the bubbling fizz of drinks.
I will put into my precious box the generousness of spending
          money on others.
I will put into my precious box the friendship, happiness,
          laughter and kind personalities of my friends.
I will put into my precious box the exciting life in my house.
I will put into my precious box the feeling good and warmth
          of my clothes.
I will put into my precious box the good memories and closeness
          of my teddy.
I will put into my precious box the comfort and dreams that
          are tucked inside my bed.
I will put into my precious box the important communication
          locked up in my phone.

I will not put into my precious box the scary, frightening dreams
that have gone wrong and turned into nightmares.
I will not put into my precious box the winding up into a yo-yo that
comes from the annoyance of my brother.
I will not put into my precious box the sickly juice and taste
          of a tomato.
I will not put into my precious box the decorated material of dresses.
I will not put into my precious box the slimy disgusting skin of big
          and small snails.

Katie Whytock (11)
South Leys School

MY PRECIOUS BOX

I will put into my precious box the kindness, care, love and also the
annoyance of my family.
I will put into my precious box the warmth and relaxing feel of
my house.

I will put into my precious box the taste and satisfaction of food.
I will put into my precious box the entertaining drama of my TV.

I will put into my precious box the music and entertainment of
my stereo.
I will put into my precious box the comfort and reusability of CDs.

I will put into my precious box the friendliness and companionship
of my friends.
I will put into my precious box the playfulness and cuddliness of
my rabbit.

I will put into my precious box the communications of my mobile.
I will put into my precious box the taste and melting feel
of chocolate.

I will not put into my precious box the long legs and hairy bodies
of spiders.
I will not put into my precious box the feeling of butterflies
in my stomach.

I will not put into my precious box the colour and taste of mushy peas.
I will not put the awful feeling of when I fall over in front of everyone.

Karen Kirkby (11)
South Leys School

DARKNESS

Darkness is my only friend yet my only enemy,
It is in the eyes of people I meet.
They stare blankly at me,
Their dagger-like eyes penetrating my flesh,
Their cold words exceed my expectations,
The numerous ways I can deal with it.
Yet, I choose abruptly,
Some day there will be someone beside me
To tell me what to do,
Help me decide,
I hope someday I will find someone like you,
Someone to hold me in the night,
Someone to show there is something other than darkness.
The darkness that surrounds me and engulfs me,
Seems to tear at my soul,
The darkness inside me,
The darkness I see,
The thing that will save me is your love for me.

Samantha Markham (13)
South Leys School

PRECIOUS BOX POETRY

In my precious box I will put;
The delicious taste of juicy pizza
running down my chin.
The taste of nutty and creamy juicy chocolate.
A friend to talk to, and to laugh with.
Tyne, Tess, loyal, kind and loving
and always there to protect me.
My make-up, because it makes me feel
groovy and funky.

Courtney Butterfield (11)
South Leys School

MY PRECIOUS BOX

I will put into my precious box the fresh, watery
juice of a long, brown sausage from a hot dog.

I will not put into my precious box the ugly smell
of my bin.

I will not put into my precious box the brightness
of my bedroom.

I will not put into my precious box the nastiness
of my brothers.

I will put into my precious box the huge bounce
of my football.

I will not put into my precious box the annoyance
of my sister.

Scott Mackenzie (11)
South Leys School

PRECIOUS BOX POETRY

The warmness of my duvet
which I tuck in every night
and the smell of my mum's cooking
which tastes better every day.
The cosy comfort of my sofa
that sits there in the lounge
and the voices of my friends
playing out on the street
and the barking of my dog every time
somebody knocks on our door.

Karis McIlwain (11)
South Leys School

MY PRECIOUS BOX

I will put into my precious box the tender loving care of my family.
I will put into my precious box the fun and happiness of playing
                                                    with my friends.
I will put into my precious box the warmth and privacy of my bedroom.
I will put into my precious box the cheering of the football club
                                            and fans at the game.
I will put into the precious box the taste of colourful sweets.

I will not put into my precious box the freezing cold weather.
I will not put into my box the Scunthorpe United football team.
I will not put into my box the loudness of people shouting.
I will not put into my box the soreness of cuts from falling over.

Rachel Jarvis (11)
South Leys School

PRECIOUS BOX POETRY

Into my precious box I will put;

My mum because she feeds me,
washes my clothes and she loves me.

My dad because he takes me
where I want to go and he loves me.

My sister Daniella because I will miss her.

My memories of my sister (Sammy)
because I will miss them.

My grandma, because I can look after her
because she is ill.

My grandads because I love them.

Jessica Batchelor (11)
South Leys School

GOD BLESS YOU NOW

To a wonderful husband
To you a loving wife
To my purest children
The best things in my life
To a beautiful sister
My love will never end
To my caring brother
To you my silent friend.

A moment of silence
Full of deepest prayers
Hoping you can hear us
Hoping you are there
No one could imagine
The tears we've cried
We join here in song now
To bid our goodbyes.

Tears when we watched you go
Leaving us here to grieve
The memory of you will stay
Though you will have to leave
We will always be here with you
And we'll always pray
Soon we will join you
At Heaven's open gates.

To a wonderful husband
To you a loving wife
To my purest children
The best things in my life
To a beautiful sister
No love will ever end
To my caring brother
To you my silent friend.

Clare Robinson (15)
South Leys School

MY PRECIOUS BOX

I will put into my precious box the comedian antics of my pet dog.
I will put into my precious box the sympathy and softness
                                        of my teddies.
I will put into my precious box the love and annoyance of my family.
I will put into my precious box the kindness and happiness
                                        of my friends.
I will put into my precious box the warmth and cosiness of my bed.
I will put into my precious box the softness and comfort of my chair.
I will put into my precious box the finely tuned polishing
                                        of my hairbrush.
I will put into my precious box the competitive challenges
                                of my PlayStation.

I will not put in my precious box the smelliness and uncleanliness
                                of my dustbin.
I will not put in my precious box the annoyance of my little sister.
I will not put in my precious box the gnats in the bushes in our garden.
I will not put in my precious box the bossiness of Davina Dowling.

Emily McCleave (11)
South Leys School

My Precious Box

I will put into my precious box the love and kindness of my family.
I will put into my precious box the fun and laughter of my friends.
I will put into my precious box the excitement of Liverpool
                                            football team.
I will put into my precious box my own space and the privateness
                                            of my own room.
I will put into my precious box the comfort and softness of my teddy.
I will put into my precious box the entertaining interest of my TV.
I will put in my precious box the taste and fullness of food.
I will put into my precious box the fun and interest of my laptop.
I will put into my precious box the contact of my family from
                                            my mobile.
I will put in my precious box the trend and colours of my clothing.
I will put in my precious box the comfyness and style of my
                                            shoes or trainers.
I will put in my precious box the freshness and taste of drinks.

I will not put in my precious box the mean and cruel things that
                                            people do (nasty people).
I will not put in my precious box the loudness that makes me
                                            lose concentration.
I will not put in my precious box the coldness and thunder
and lightning of the horrible weather.
I will not put in my precious box the sad feelings I get when I'm hurt.

Bethany Simpson (12)
South Leys School

STAR SIGNS

My star sign is Libra, the scales
Which means I can wish for big whales,
Or look in the sky and suddenly see
A star that's shaped like you and me.

Here is the sign of Pisces the fish
If cooked properly they make a good dish,
It can be cod or haddock, whatever with chips
I'm sure it will make you lick your lips.

We're Gemini and we are the twins
We eat anything as long as it's in tins,
We stay together and enjoy the fun
And then part when the day is done.

This is Sagittarius and he's often called Cupid
He's called that when his arrows land somewhere stupid,
If hit by an arrow you'll fall in love soon,
Make sure it's a prince, not a baboon.

Next is Cancer the crab
Who might sometimes feel a little drab,
They can live in sea or sand
Which to them is a magical land.

Then Scorpio the scorpion
Who likes to have a bit of fun,
His favourite place is in the sea
And likes to swim like you and me.

Kirsty Berry (12)
Spilsby King Edward VI School

CONSTELLATION CONFRONTATION

Aries, Taurus, Gemini, Cancer
Leo, Virgo, Scorpio as well
Pick from Sagittarius, Capricorn
Which one are you? Now you have to tell.
Libra, Aquarius, Pisces, all three are noble and true,
Stick with these and you will find a friend who'll stay with you.
Leos are show-offs,
Libras are smart,
Pisces are fishy,
Geminis have heart,
Taurus are feisty,
Cancer are kind,
Virgo are organised,
Scorpio are clever of mind,
Sagittarius and Aquarius
Are both brave and loyal.
Capricorn and Aries
Prance around as if they're royal
Born under your star sign
You wield its characteristics
Half the things you read aren't true,
So don't rely on mystics
So now we've covered astrology.
Look out for your constellation,
None of its mythology
So find it without hesitation.

Holly Hardiman & Lydia Cartwright (13)
Spilsby King Edward VI School

ZODIAC POEM

The moon is in Aquarius.
Or maybe it's in Mars?
Wherever it might be,
See the future in your stars.
Twelve signs there are to choose from,
And destiny chooses in your stars,
The time, the date, the place,
Revealing who you really are.

Ellyce Coote (11)
Spilsby King Edward VI School

ZODIAC

Z odiac: the mysterious stars
O n a clear night sky the constellations shine but by
D ay the stars still shine but are invisible.
I n the cold night sky the moon glitters like gems
A nd the constellations come to life.
C an you find your future?

Christian Gunson (12)
Spilsby King Edward VI School

ZODIAC

Z odiac's the sign of earth, wind and fire,
O verall predictions could be your desire,
D esires are seen by those with the sight,
I n all the predictions some may be right,
A strologers study the stars so bright,
C lairvoyants are known to have the sight.

Staceyanne Huskisson (11)
Spilsby King Edward VI School

MY ZODIAC POEM

These are signs of the zodiac, each one for a month of the year.

Aries, the ram has curly horns used for butting,
Taurus, the bull is large and fierce.
Gemini, twins play happily together,
Cancer, the crab has sharp pincers that nip,
Leo, the lion has a long mane and a loud roar.
Virgo, the virgin is pure and white,
Libra is there to keep the balance.
Scorpio has a sting in its tail to use if it is attacked.
Sagittarius, will shoot arrows,
Capricorn, the goat is stubborn and eats all it sees.
Aquarius, will carry the water to drink,
Pisces, the fishes will swim in the salty sea.

Nicola Coupland (11)
Spilsby King Edward VI School

ZODIAC

S   agittarians are kind and thoughtful,
A   lways busy and quick.
G   iving, sharing and very fit,
I   f they hurt someone or do something wrong they always apologise.
T   hey like to have lots of friends
T   ry to help others in need,
A   ries and Leo they get along with best.
R   eally give everything the best shot.
I   f they get annoyed they can get bad-tempered.
U   nited with the sun sign of fire.
S   ay no and they will accept no for an answer.

Todd Stuart-Fawkes (11)
Spilsby King Edward VI School

THE ZODIAC

The signs of the spring let happiness in.

Aries the ram fathers a lamb
Taurus the bull eats 'til he's full
Gemini the twins watch new life begin.

The signs of the sun bring heat, joy and fun.

Cancer the crab thinks beaches are fab
Leo the lion - in the sun's rays he's lying
Virgo the maid keeps cool in the shade.

The signs of the fall ask the north wind to call.

Libra the scales hears the wind when it wails
Scorpio the scorpion fears the bonfire beside her
Sagittarius the archer keeps warm in his armchair.

The signs of the snow make our rosy cheeks glow.

Capricorn the goat wears a thick winter coat
Aquarius brings water, a gift for his daughter
Pisces the fish brings a magical wish.

So a year has gone by.

And now we are back
We begin once again
With a new zodiac.

Katy Holmes (13)
Spilsby King Edward VI School

THE ZODIAC

The zodiac has twelve signs
to keep us on the right lines.
The first sign is Aquarius
bringing water for all of us.
The second is Pisces,
the fish of the seas.
Now is Aries the ram
he likes mint sauce with his lamb!
Taurus the bull
gives the warning call.
Fifth is Gemini,
the twins say 'Hi.'
Next is Cancer, the crab,
he never looks drab.
Leo the lion
never puts his tie on!
Eighth is Virgo, the girl,
she wears a pretty pearl.
Libra the scales
are too small for whales.
Next comes Scorpio the spider,
she makes a web beside her.
Sagittarius shoots his arrow,
watch out for that sparrow!
Next is Capricorn the pretty goat,
she wears a pretty coat.
They are the twelve signs of the zodiac,
wait until next year, they'll be back!

Leanne Holmes (11)
Spilsby King Edward VI School

Zodiac Poem

The black sky at night
with the stars twinkling bright
Tell us what the future might be.
Some people believe
and some people don't.
Horoscopes can be wrong
or they can be right.
Watch your stars float by,
right up high in the black sky,
and ask yourself,
'Why, oh why?'
Your love life, relationships
and lucky number,
can be told from a bright
little wonder.

Georgina Crust (12)
Spilsby King Edward VI School

The Zodiac

Zodiac is mysterious and not yet clear to us,
It could hide our future or a load of nonsense.
Sagittarius and Aquarius, Pisces too,
Capricorn and Cancer or is it Virgo?
Libra or Leo or could it be Scorpio?
Or possibly Aries? Taurus? Gemini?
Whatever you are; do you think it's true?
Well that's up to you!

John Maycock (11)
Spilsby King Edward VI School

SCORPIO

Very reliable and always fair,
Playing freely, not a care,
Independent you will stand,
Being generous and grand.

Prospers greatly through the years,
Helping others with no fears,
Always do as you are told,
Are very brave, big and bold.

Amongst the others stand out proud,
Yet hang around with the crowd,
You will continue to be a leader,
And halt to help a desperate pleader.

In the rough you are the diamond,
Never were a Simple Simon,
Forever onward, a high achiever,
Not a very big believer.

Very polite and well-mannered,
If you meet one you are sure to be enamoured,
Wisely chooses all your friends,
Always quick to make amends.

In the countryside you play all day,
No one takes your joy away,
Can be shy, quiet and retired,
But watch out if you get fired.

Marching onward down the road of success,
That's one great person that you can't depress,
A lover of music and almost all sound,
The bearer of courage that knows no bounds.

Scorpios are renowned for their humour,
And pay no heed to a nasty rumour.

Kristi Fothergill (11)
Spilsby King Edward VI School

THE ZODIAC TRAIN

'All aboard the zodiac train,'
See animals of the unexplained
The frightening Leo, the luscious Libra,
How 'bout glimpsing captivating Cancer?
Does the cantering Capricorn take your fancy?

Testing Taurus, pleasing Pisces splashing in the sea.
'All aboard the zodiac train.'
Are you the same star sign as me?

Dive underwater with aqua Aquarius,
And take a deep breath for me.
Scuttle the sting with scary Scorpio,
Mystical creatures from the deep blue sea.

Step right on the train of love,
'Cause saucy Sagittarius came from above,
The Gemini twins keep our hearts aglow
When we came and met the gorgeous Virgo.

Last but not least, we have our Aries,
Although we come in different varieties,
We all show our love and care,
Are you coming aboard or staying there?

Jessica Tilley (14)
Spilsby King Edward VI School

THE STARS

Last night I looked up at the sky,
Round about half-past ten.
I saw a new bright light up there,
And wondered where it had been.

Did it see the galaxy,
Or the Milky Way?
Did it see a meteor
in passing on its way?

It must have taken light years
To get to where it is,
To shine so bright with others,
Up in the dark night sky.

Louise Johnson (12)
Spilsby King Edward VI School

DREAMLAND

My eyes light up like a midnight star
I dance through the night with my music on
I want to work at Butlin's
To wear that red coat and be a helper.

But first I want to do well at school
To do my best at all my work
I will try my best to reach my goal
And try to be on top every day.

When my SATS have gone by
I will be ready for my next ones
To be at my best, that's what I need to be
To be a DJ or even be myself.

Ashley Kirby (12)
George Farmer Technology College

A FIGHT

After a drink or two in the local inn
We all go outside where a fight is going to begin
Eyes everywhere
A horrible stare. Hold on!
The fight is about to start.
A whoosh and swoop and a hit and a tap
Fist and hands flying everywhere
Without any care
A cheer and a boo and an aye or a nay
The people who are fighting
Don't care what they say
All of a sudden it goes quiet
The fight is over
Let's get back to the inn.

Thomas Chapman (15)
George Farmer Technology College

A BAD DAY

A s I get tired

B ad will come
A s I get bored
D ays become years

D etentions become boredom
A ttention no more
Y es! I am home at last.

Robert Spriggs (12)
George Farmer Technology College

SAD I AMS

I am
The blunt pin
Pushed in the ceiling
The scraps
Of chips had for tea
The newspaper
With last year's news.

I am
The wasp
With no sting
The ball with no air
The crumpled rubber, the inkless pen
The ruler
With no numbers
The dishes
That you forgot
To clean.

I am
The book with pages gone
The paper that is ripped
The bulb with no light
The toothbrush with no bristles
The vacuum that exploded
The sun that forgot to shine.

I am
A library
With a few books
A pen
That's never been used
The jeans
No one wants to wear
A mum with advice
That her kids ignore.

Laura-Jo Baldwin (12)
George Farmer Technology College

FOOTBALL

The crowds wait patiently for their team.
The teams come out of the tunnel.
The crowds roar with excitement.
The teams get ready in their formation.
A team of eleven is standing in their magnificent colours.
The whistle blows and the game begins.
The aim of the game is for one of the teams to score some goals.
The crowds chant and sing to spur on their team.
They roar and the stadium thunders when a goal is scored.
When the 90th minute passes the whistle blows bringing the
game to an end.
There can only be a win, a lose or a draw each game.
Celebrations and sorrow,
For some, an end to a perfect day as they make their way home.
All this happens in a season of what is known as football.

Luke Webb (11)
George Farmer Technology College

CRICKET

As I walk to he crease
With the bat in my hand
I survey my surroundings
Before I take my stand.

The crowd watch my every step I make
I'm scared that I'll cause a mistake.

The ball flies towards me at a speeding pace.
I use my bat to shield my face.

Whack! Goes the ball leather against willow.
I go to run and my legs feel like concrete pillars.

Faster/faster I have to run
To reach the other side,
I can't go slowly and abide my time.

Ashley Godfrey (15)
George Farmer Technology College

FLOWERS

Flowers small, flowers bright,
Flowers shining in the midsummer
Nights.
I wish, I will, I wish, I might, wish upon you
Tonight
The wish I wish is for you to see
The perfect side of the perfect
Me!

Sarah Thwaites (11)
George Farmer Technology College

PE Lesson

Skip and jump all lesson
It causes lots of sweat and depression
Run around the footie pitch
Make sure you don't fall in the ditch

Bounce a ball up and down
Kick a ball, round and round
Jump up high into the sky
Like you are trying to fly

Play a game of footie in the wet
You are going to get soaked - I bet
Getting dressed is the best
In the dry, forget the rest.

George Spencer (11)
George Farmer Technology College

What Am I?

Lurking in muddy shadows deep,
On unsuspecting prey I peep,
Two beads of saffron glow bright as day,
Waiting for my chance to play.

My jagged back skims along,
My emerald scales, my tail so long,
A graceful killer with jaws of white,
Like spikes of broken glass shine in the light.

So can you guess what I am?
Am I bird or fish or man?
No other creature has my smile,
Of course I am a crocodile.

Ryan Clayton (14)
George Farmer Technology College

OUT ON THE STREETS

It was as scary as a jack-o'-lantern at Hallowe'en,
Never knowing what was round the corner
Never knowing if you would live to fight another day
It is now September, it is getting colder.

I am as cold as a cold-hearted demon from Hell,
My bottom is as numb as antiseptic
You try and try to get to sleep
But all you can feel is the numbness in your feet.

You're as penniless as a student at university,
You get hungrier and hungrier
You get more and more thirsty
But all you can think about is your home in the city.

I am as black as a witch's hair flying through the midnight sky
I smell like a skunk
And look like a punk
After all I am just trash to them.

Ben Adams (13)
George Farmer Technology College

LEAVING SCHOOL

In year 6, it's our last day,
Packing up our stuff to go away,
Who is my next teacher? Who? Oh who?
Leaving school, boo hoo hoo.

Starting a new school again,
Like a storm with lots of rain,
Moving round from class to class,
At lunch, picking my nose on the grass.

Not talking in our test,
Trying to get best marks, please be the best,
Settled down and in gear,
July is the date, end of year.

Zoe Rowlett (13)
George Farmer Technology College

MY STREET LIFE

I'm cold as a can of Coke
Straight from the fridge
I watch people walk by in big coats and scarves
I wish I was warm.
I wish.

I'm as hungry as a starving cat.
I'm longing for food.
People pass eating burgers and chips.
I wish I was eating.
I wish.

I'm ragged as a derelict building.
People pass with nice clothes and combed hair.
I wish I was dressed nicely.
I wish.

I'm lonely as a lot of sheep
All cold and alone in the big, wide world.
I'm hungry, starving and ragged
I wish I was like other people.
I wish.

Hannah Thorpe (13)
George Farmer Technology College

I HAVEN'T A CLUE

Here I sit upon my bed
I've got to write a poem,
How do I start?
How do I finish?
What's the subject?
What's the plot?
I just really don't know.

I could write about football
But my mates will do that.
I could write about school,
But what's there to tell?
Oh please help me, what can I do?

I glance at the clock
Time is going fast.
I'm yawning well and feeling sleepy
Please help me, I haven't a clue.

Tom Louth (14)
George Farmer Technology College

HUNGRY

My stomach churns like an engine
Getting hungrier each day
I am wasting away here
On my spot on the pavement

Time is as slow as a snail
The hours slowly tick by
But when day turns to night,
The hours turn colder.

Rich people go into shops like
Bees to a honey pot,
But they have no time for me
Some do give, but most don't.

As happy as a clown
I go to the bar
For my plate of chips.
I'm not hungry anymore.

Eric Forbes-Whitmore (13)
George Farmer Technology College

HOW I ENVY THEM

It's as cold as a freezer.
The people are walking by with
woolly hats and woolly coats
while I'm sitting here wrapped
in my sleeping bag.
How I envy them so.

I feel as dirty as mud,
I see people walking in the streets,
lovely and clean but they still moan.
My hair is horrible and greasy,
I really want to wash it and have a bath
but I can't.
How I envy them so.

As loud as a police siren,
That's what the drunks are like
when they come out of the pubs,
and start laughing at me and having fun.
How I envy them so.

Laura Wells (13)
George Farmer Technology College

HOW I FEEL ABOUT BEING HOMELESS

I'm as cold as an icy river
With no warmth
It makes me shiver,
Sometimes I have no shelter
My clothes are worn too
But no one thinks about that.

I feel as lonely as the sun in the sky
As people walk by
No one gives you a second thought
Or they stop and stare
I miss my family and friends,
But no one loves me.

I sleep on a bed like pebbles
It's cold and damp
When I move I get bruises.
I always ache
Sleeping is nearly impossible
But no one cares about me.

Sometimes I feel starved like a lion,
I have to beg for money,
I only feed once a day.
Sometimes I eat nothing -
It depresses me.
I wish someone would love me.

Claire Venni (13)
George Farmer Technology College

SLOWLY

I was as black as ink.
I had to use public toilets for a wash.
I had to watch clean people walk by,
Why couldn't I be clean too?

Getting money was like getting water
                        out of a rock.
Some people would stare,
Others just walk away,
But most just look down their noses at me.

I felt like I had been sleeping in a freezer.
The nights were so long and cold,
The floor was so hard,
I was hurting all over.

Time went so slow, every minute
                    seemed like a lifetime.
I watched people go by,
They didn't have a care in the world.
There aren't enough hours in the day for them
But for me
Life continues
To go
Slow
Slow
Slowly
        by!

Emma Barber (13)
George Farmer Technology College

WHO CARES?

My hair is as greasy as a chip fryer,
While everyone else is so lovely and clean,
While I long for just a wash and clean,
I use public toilets for a wash, for a small amount of money,
But haven't washed for months now.
People make me feel bad, upsetting,
When they describe me as a dirty toilet.

I'm as penniless as a newborn baby
Wondering when will be my next tea,
Wondering if anyone will drop me a few silvers,
                              for a pot of tea.
Thinking of those people walking past in woolly coats
And driving flash cars.
I hate that feeling that nobody cares,
The only place I can afford that will always be there
                              is the bins.

I'm as cold as a cube,
I lie on my sleeping bag at night,
My pack as my cushion,
I envy people who take clothes for granted,
I'm as cold as anything, thinking of people in
                              nice warm beds,
I sit here with a withered-away T-shirt
And a torn pair of joggers?
    Does anyone care?

I'm as sad as a slave,
I sit here at Kings Cross.
As bored as anything,
Wondering what else could possibly go wrong,
Wondering if I'll ever have job,

Wondering would anyone care if I disappeared,
Does anyone care?
I wish I was like others,
I wish so badly.

Nikita Richardson (13)
George Farmer Technology College

A LONELY LIFE

The night is as gloomy as the look on my face.
I'm lonely and afraid as I look into space.
Here I am, alone on the step.
I wish I was tucked up in my nice, warm bed.

I'm as hungry as a horse.
I could do with a good feed.
Here I am begging.
Please let me eat.

My face is as black as coal.
My body's just as bad.
My hair needs a good wash,
And my clothes are just rags.

Time goes by as slow as a tortoise.
Days just drag on.
Nights are just as long.
But time will slowly go on.

I'm as scared as a kitten.
Scared I will fall,
I know some day my time will come,
But until then I am grateful for all I have.

Emma-Jane Williams (13)
George Farmer Technology College

NIGHT

It's as black as the moon
It's as dark as dark can be
You hear things, they scare you.

It's as cold as stone
The floor sends shivers down your spine
You always have goosebumps.

It's as dark as the darkest night
You are scared because of the creatures
The things that go bump in the night.

It's as loud as the howl of a wolf
I hear them, they speak to me
They're going to get me, they tell me so.

It's as light as a sunrise
The dark is going now, the things, the dark, the moon
They've gone but they will be back tonight.

Tom Fathers (14)
George Farmer Technology College

MY FAMILY

My family are really nice
They treat me with care
I live with my mum, my dad and my sister.
My nan and grandad live behind.

I look like my dad,
He's big-built because he's a builder.
At weekends he goes up the pub
My dad works late
So I hardly ever see him.

My mum works for Nestlé chocolate
We get loads of it.
Mum comes home early in the day.
My mum goes up the pub too.

My sister just goes out with her friends.

Lana Hughes (11)
George Farmer Technology College

SEA

Life goes up and down
Like the sea
I see little fishes
Trying to swim free

The sea is the greatest
Thing of all
The big waves rise up
Just like a wall

The tides move in
And out
On the seabed
I see a trout

I looked out
Into sea
Is that a trout
Looking up at me?

I look out to sea
And sea the sunset
I may keep a fish
As a pet?

Shane Hughes (14)
George Farmer Technology College

OUT ON THE STREETS

As homeless as a stray dog
I'm out on the streets,
Nowhere to go.
Searching for food.

The floor is as hard as rock
I can't get to sleep.
I feel all numb,
Twisting and turning,
I can't get to sleep.

It's as cold as snow
I can't get warm,
My clothes are wet and dirty,
Wait, someone please help me!

I'm as hungry as a starving person
Searching for food
Asking for money but never getting much.
Rummaging through dustbins,
Screaming, 'Feed me, feed me!'

Darren Callister (14)
George Farmer Technology College

MY KITTEN

Smooth, silky fur,
Pointy, fluffy ears,
Sweet, cute, little pink nose,
She always purrs when you hug her.

Sparkling, shimmering eyes that glow in the dark,
Walks proudly round with her tail up high
Runs like the wind or crouches down low,
Chasing birds, she loves it so.

Playful as a baby
Miaows softly but loud.
Can stand on two legs,
She looks very proud.

She sits and waits as still as night,
In the dark for birds in flight.
Her name is Tazmin, or Puss to you,
But to me she will always be my best friend, Taz.

Kelsey Candler (12)
George Farmer Technology College

LOVE?

These weird feelings are whizzing round me,
I don't know what it is or what to do,
I have a special person though,
He makes me feel so happy,
It's kinda just like a roller coaster,
You know,
You go up and down,
Round and round,
You feel dizzy,
But it's just so exciting!
You never want to stop!
Sometimes it does stop though,
It never always goes right,
Your heart is broken
Into little pieces,
You feel like it can never be mended,
The roller coaster is gone,
But not forever.

Kerry Lashmar (13)
George Farmer Technology College

DO YOU CARE?

I have the same amount of money as an animal.
I sit here in Trafalgar Square begging for money.
Will I be able to afford a cup of tea before the end of the day?

Do you care?

I am as cold as an ice cream,
Night is the hardest time of all.
The floor is so hard and cold.
Not had a good night's sleep for ages.
I just lie and listen to the cars going by.

Do you care?

I am as hungry as a crocodile
I haven't eaten for days now.
I normally have a pizza now and then.
Don't have much money, you see.
Sometimes people leave some nice food
in the bins for me to eat.

Do you care?

Time goes as slowly as a snail!
I just sit day after day watching the people walk by,
Trying not to make eye contact with me.
I sit and wonder what I am doing here?
Why did I leave my mum and dad?

Do they care?

Amy Cooke (13)
George Farmer Technology College

NOBODY LOVES ME

It's hard living on the streets like in London, I mean
The time goes by as slowly as a tortoise
Some people give, some people don't,
Others act as if they've not heard your voice.
I have nobody to love me.

The summer is warm
As hot as an oven even
You get in your sleeping bag and you sweat an ocean
I have nobody to love me.

The winter is cold
As cold as a freezer
You get in your sleeping bag thinking you are
Going to be warm but you're just like an icicle.
I have nobody to love me.

In winter your sleeping bag
Is as cold as a snowball
You know you're going to get colder
I have nobody to love me.

The evenings are scary
The nights as scary as a witch
The shadows are scarier than Medusa
I have nobody to love me.

Breakfast time is lovely
The breakfast is as warm as a radiator
But later I have to go begging
I have nobody to love me.

Matthew Dean (14)
George Farmer Technology College

AFRAID

Homelessness is like turning a corner then nothing's there,
Like a ghost that passes through you,
It's a cold feeling, colder than ice,
You can't look back or your heart bleeds,
And you want to turn back.

Night-time is like a nightmare,
You never fully go to sleep or you'll never wake up again,
Different dossers take things from you,
When this happens you think 'I'm going to get you back.'

Dossing is like looking for a needle in a haystack,
When you think you've got something, it just falls away,
You're hoping all the time you'll get a lucky break.

Trying to find a friend is like trying to win the lottery,
You keep buying a ticket, thinking you'll win,
But then you find out it's bad luck once again.

Simon Waters (14)
George Farmer Technology College

SHOPPING WITH MY MUM

Shopping with my mum,
Is why I feel so glum.
Around the shops we go,
As my anger grows.

In and out of Queensgate,
As I have to wait,
That's why I feel so glum,
Shopping with my mum.

As I try to nudge,
My mum just will not budge,
That's why I feel so glum,
Shopping with my mum.

I make my sister scream,
My mum says 'Don't be mean,'
That's why I feel so glum,
Shopping with my mum.

Joe Myles (13)
George Farmer Technology College

ON THE STREETS

Homelessness is as boring as a circus with no clowns.
When people turn the corner, just look at you and frown.
Sitting in a shop door, waiting for the light,
Too scared to go to sleep in case something gets you in the night.

Searching through dustbins like a hungry, dirty fox.
Sitting in the corner wrapped in a cardboard box,
People walk past with money flowing out of their pockets.
They just walk past, sometimes running like rockets.

The time is as slow as a slug just gone by,
You wish you were at home, warm and dry
You can't go back there, they don't appreciate you,
But then again, they're the only ones that do.

My pack is as heavy as a two-ton weight
My life was decided like a dead fish on a plate.
Do I die, live or not?
Don't leave home, it's all you've got.

Simon Eva (13)
George Farmer Technology College

THE FOUR SEASONS

It's spring, it's spring, its spring,
The flowers are peeking through the ground.
The lambs are frolicking in the fields,
The bees are buzzing around the blossom.
The trees are bursting out in leaves,
It's time to cut the lawn.

Summer's here at last,
The sun is shining bright.
Dreams of holidays by the sea,
The trees are swaying in the breeze.
The flowers are in full bloom
Midgets are crawling all over me,
It's time to cut the lawn.

Autumn's here, it's cooling down,
The leaves are turning red, gold and brown.
Rain is falling hard and cool
Fireworks are exploding in the air.
The wind is blowing very hard
The birds are ready to migrate,
It's time to cut the lawn.

Winter is here again,
It's time for the snow to come.
The ice covers everywhere,
Fires are burning in the home.
It will soon be Christmas,
At last I've put the mower away.

David Almey (12)
George Farmer Technology College

SCHOOL

Do I like school?
Well, yes and no.
Sometimes it's cool,
Sometimes it goes slow.

Teachers try to make lessons fun,
Which is great.
But there are just some subjects,
I really hate.

Games I find hard,
I'm not athletic.
But I'm sure in time,
I'll come to like it.

At dinner time some children queue up,
For hot food.
And others will push in,
Which I find quite rude.

Some homework I am given,
Can be interesting to do.
But then other times,
I don't always know what to do.

Just hope for the best,
Hope to get it right.
And not receive a warning,
That could lead to a detention at night.

Emma Richardson (12)
George Farmer Technology College

RUNNING RAIN

Running through the coldish wind,
Eyes barely open.
The wind whistling around,
What an awful sound.

I cantered along through the wood,
So peaceful that I stood.
As I stood the rain dripped through,
I ran as fast as I could.

I walked across the field as the rain,
Pattered to the ground.
My hooves splashed in puddles,
Time to find my nice warm stable,
And my full feeding bag.
Hee, hee, hee!

Elise Rickett (11)
George Farmer Technology College

FRIENDS

I met my friends at Primary School,
When we were only four,
I had such fun with everyone
Till I shut my fingers in the door.

We did our lessons,
Then went out to play,
After dinner we had another session,
Later we came home after a busy day.

Ben Lee (11)
George Farmer Technology College

MY WORLD

Leave me in my world,
Let me dream,
In this world things aren't as they seem.
I don't want to wake up to reality,
Because I will end up losing my sanity.

Don't wake up,
I like this land,
Leave me here,
Where I'll stand.
Here things are happy,
They aren't sad,
Nothing happens which is bad.

My time will come when I'll wake,
I'm not sailing on a peaceful lake.
My dream is over,
My dream has gone,
But my life still carries on.

Kate Atkinson (15)
George Farmer Technology College

A BAD DAY

Sometimes I get   A ngry

Because I am   B ored
I then get   A ggressive
And do some   D amage

It makes me feel   D epressed
Inside I am   A fraid
                      Y uk!

Lewis Ashley Forman (12)
George Farmer Technology College

I'M SO SORRY!

On Christmas Eve
At half-past twelve,
I got my golf clubs off the shelf.
Then off we went,
My friend and I,
To use the golf clubs,
Or at least try.
She put the ball upon the tee,
But it all went wrong,
And she hit me.
The tears came up,
The blood came down,
And then I fell upon the ground.
Next thing I was on a bed,
With stitches coming out my head.
I looked at my friend.
She looked at me.
Then she said.
'I'm so sorry!'

Rebecca Wright (13)
George Farmer Technology College

ANGRY

Sometimes I get   A   ngry when

People   B   reak promises
Then I get an   A   ttitude problem
And I   D   are to react

And I feel   D   ejected and
I am all   A   lone and
I wish it was   Y   esterday.

Chris Ingle (12)
George Farmer Technology College

MY SISTER

She had her whole life in front of her,
A free spirit, some might say,
Just left school at sweet sixteen,
A bit lonely in the day.

She had someone special to rely on,
So special they got engaged,
Then there was another commitment,
They were over the moon that day.

Her temper became less noticeable,
Smiling day in and day out,
She looked as fresh as spring,
With a natural shine.

Then it came along one morning,
Family came to visit,
Everyone was full of joy,
On the arrival of a baby boy.

Catherine Griggs (14)
George Farmer Technology College

A BAD DAY

A   lways alone

B   ecause I have no friends
A   ngry and alone
D   anger around the corner

D   isappointed
A   lienated and
Y   earning for friends.

Scott Fitzjohn (12)
George Farmer Technology College

SAD I AMS

I am
the handle
from the broken mug
the flowers
from which the smell has gone
the knife
with which the blade is blunt.
I am
the teddy
with no cuddle
the sun
without its heat
and the dog
without his bark.
I am
the fire
without any flames
the book
with no words
the baby
with no cry.
I am
the sea
without any water
the mirror
without any reflection
and the clock
with no tick.

I am
the heart
with no blood
the body
with no soul
the Earth
without its core.

Jessica Stuffins (12)
George Farmer Technology College

THE FOX IN THE NIGHT

It hunts in the blackness of the night
Running from tree to tree.
Sticking to the shadow of the night sky.

The light of the pale moon shines on the
Thick red fur to make his presence known
To the man who hunts him.

As he swiftly moves towards his prey
Not a sound passes his lips. He treads like
A mouse ever so softly.

Closer, closer and then without a sound
He attacks its prey lunging into the
Chicken's neck
Biting into the windpipe.

The chicken takes its final breath and dies in the
Fox's mouth. Dragging the limp body of what was
A chicken through the shadows.

Through the sky on the hill the fox waits
For his next kill.

Michael Rickett (14)
George Farmer Technology College

WEDNESDAY, HOCKEY

Sigh, it's Wednesday
That means hockey,
Bet I'll get told off
'Cause sometimes I'm too cocky.

Start of 5 minute run
Calf muscles hurting,
Heart pounding,
'This is no fun.'

We start a game
I'm on the blue team,
Reds 1 point, blues, nothing
It's always the same.

Tomorrow is Thursday
No more hockey,
Until next week,
Hip, hip hooray!

Laura Anderson (13)
George Farmer Technology College

THE OUTDOORS

Kayaking is fun,
there's one to a boat
if you fall in,
you'll usually float.

Climbing is good,
it's very, very high
if you climb long enough,
you'll reach the sky.

Abseiling is fun,
it's a long way down,
but unlike canoeing,
you'll never drown.

Hiking is good,
but the walk is long,
if it's long enough,
you can sing a song.

Chris Birchall (13)
George Farmer Technology College

MY TRIP TO SPAIN

I feel the hot sun beating down on my back
I taste the flowing wine
I listen to the blue sea
I feel the breeze of the wind

The bright hot colours
The reds the yellows of flamenco dancers
I hear the sound of castanets
Beating in my ears

Sleepy siestas in the heat of the day
Water glistening from wet bodies
The smell of suntan lotion
While I walk along the soft sand

The taste of fried shrimp
With a sangria to wash it down
I sit and watch the sun set in the sky
I wish I could be there again.

Siobhan Blundell (14)
George Farmer Technology College

WHY?

My mummy thinks the world of me.
She jumps with joy and glee,
She says I'm beautiful, smart and clever.
Even when she's under the weather.
But then, oh no! What a shame!
When she went out for the day!

Her tummy's big, she's awfully fat.
Grandma's bought a brand new hat
Why?
Because of course, Mummy's having a baby
If it's a boy, she'll call it Davie
It's not fair
Mummy don't care
About *me!*

Lucy McMahon (13)
George Farmer Technology College

MY STAR

As I lay on the dew covered grass,
Looking towards the heavens,
Stars twinkled,
Dark backcloth,
Night sky.
My star, brighter than all.

Now it's gone,
And never coming back.
Vanished without a trace.
Heart longing,
Eyes stinging.
My heart aching more than ever.

Anne Horrell (14)
George Farmer Technology College

ELEPHANTS

They slowly stomp from place to place,
Big, fat and grey, they need not race,
As their tail starts to sway,
They stop and halt in water, and start to spray.

Blowing their trunks to find the pack,
Eating leaves stack by stack,
They are better in the wild, than in the zoo,
But they seem happy all day through.

They can laze about all day long,
Not a worry in the world,
Until a hunter comes along,
They shoot them down and steal their tusks,
Then leave them there from dawn till dusk.

Helen Mackinder (14)
George Farmer Technology College

A TIGER

A tiger roars all day long
A tiger has black and orange stripes
A tiger eats other animals
A tiger lives in a zoo.

Tigers love to see children
But please don't touch the
Cage or you'll lose your fingers
So if you're bored why not get your parents
To take you to the zoo, to see your favourite animal?

Holly Dickinson (14)
George Farmer Technology College

THERE'S NOTHING WITH ME OR MY FAMILY

I get picked on in school,
People say I'm unfashionable,
Well at least I don't write on my table,
Or sit around watching cable.

People say I'm too quiet,
Or my sister needs to go on a diet,
But I don't care because my dad fixes pylons,
And my auntie makes clothes using silks and nylons.

People say, 'Why do you always get an A.'
I reply, 'Well I don't worry about how I look all day.'
When it comes to animals people say I have a special way,
I even buy my horses fresh hay.

I put up with all this every day.

Sarah Ryan (13)
George Farmer Technology College

THE DOLPHIN

Clash clash
Splash splash.
Kept in a cage with no escape
People stare, stare and watch.

No escape
No door.
Kept inside
Wall after wall.

Like a man in a box
His anger shows.
Stranded and starved
But his efforts are to no avail.

Big Tom they call him
The people's hero.
They think he lives like a king
Fame who needs it?

Carl Newell (14)
George Farmer Technology College

BEST FRIENDS

Best friends are like good books,
You don't always use them,
But when you need them,
You know where to find them.

Best friends are like boyfriends,
You don't always love them,
But when you need them,
You know where to find them.

Best friends you love them,
You care for them,
You don't always need them,
But they know you care.

Best friends are like . . .
Nothing else but *best friends.*

Tina Paske (14)
George Farmer Technology College

SAD I AMS

I am
the shell
from a shrivelled-up snail.
The teddy
that nobody loves.
The shoe
without a sole.

I am
the fur
unwanted by a rabbit.
The lens
unwanted by the glasses.
The doll
unwanted by the girl.

I am
the fridge without a chill.
The light without a switch.
The phone without a ring.
The stereo without a sound.
The computer without a keyboard.
The TV without an aerial.

I am
the pen
that ran out of ink.
The book
that has ripped pages.
The pencil case
that has no pens.

I am unwanted.

Layla Black 12)
George Farmer Technology College

SAD I AMS

I am
A tree
With no leaves,
A dog with no bark,
A rose with no petals,
The flower with no scent.
I am
A milk carton with no milk,
An empty crisp packet,
I've lost my crisps.
A shop with no stock.
The cow with no moo.
I am
The wall with no bricks,
A scrap yard without scrap,
The bin with no rubbish,
A door without a lock,
A pen without ink.
I am
The shoe without a sole,
A dictionary with no words,
The sky without clouds,
A school with no children,
The mirror without a reflection.

I am not needed.

Claire Gregory (12)
George Farmer Technology College

SHARK

Like a blue flash of light
It takes a quick bite
Of a huge killer whale
It snaps at its tail.

It needs something to eat,
Perhaps blubber or meat
It does not care
It refuses to share.

When it is done
It will turn and then run
Like a dog off a lead
More food it does need.

To keep it alive
It will strive
It will swim a long way - maybe a day
To catch its prey.

Something large and grey . . .
Not seen in the light of day
It is very rare but he does not care
You can tell he is hungry by in his eyes the red flare.

He is coming so beware
He won't leave a single hair
He will have you so quick
You will not feel a prick

So if you go out into the sea
Be so very careful
Not to come into contact with me!

Mark Wiles (14)
George Farmer Technology College

WHO'S THERE?

Knock, knock, knock, someone's at the door
Knock, knock, knock, there's something under the floor.
There's something here, I am not quite sure
There's something here, it's at the door.

It's big, it's bold and it has no hold
It comes from the night to give me a fright
Knock, knock, knock, it's here tonight
I don't fear 'cause I can fight.

Knock, knock, knock,
It's coming in and I fear it will do me in
It's my mate Mark, not something from the dark
I'm a fool, now I can act cool and he will never know,
I hope he don't go!

Joe Purvis (14)
George Farmer Technology College

A FAMILY ROW

There they go again
Row - row - row
Doors slamming
Dad's shouting
My sister howling
What a mess
My mum's weeping
My brother hiding
My family is dying
A moment of silence
Then quiet.

Richard Dawson (14)
George Farmer Technology College

THE RAGING WIND

I will howl out loud on a moonlit night,
Like an owl swooping in the distance,
I will cry out loud,
Sing my song to the earth,
Like a leaf into water far away from us,
No animal or man can howl like I can,
And there is no resistance from the raging winds,
And yes before you ask no one is safe,
When I stretch out my hand and blow away the sand,
The grains of life that beseech you,
And when I go quiet,
All gentle and quiet,
A plan is cooking up inside me,
And when I fly through the air,
With a very gentle dove right beside me,
I am at peace with the earth.

David Bown (11)
The Robert Manning Technology College

A SCARY NIGHT FOR A RABBIT

Rustling in the grass as quiet as can be, a cat says 'Oh, you're nice
and tasty all for me!'
Pepper jumps as she hears the sound and tries to dig underground.
Her owner came in the deep dark night to check on her babies,
but she got a fright.
She looked on the lawn and saw her baby, then picked her up and
hugged her tight.
Owner put the baby back and tucked her in all safe and warm.
Safe from any predator that tries to disturb her from her warm bed.

Rachael Berzins (11)
The Robert Manning Technology College

It's Raining!

Pitter patter,
Water drumming on the rooftops
Pitter patter,
Water banging on the windows
Splish splash,
Water splashing in the river
Splish splash,
Water hitting the hard, dirty mud
Trickle,
Water running off the rooftops
Trickle,
Water running down the window
Thud
Bounce,
Water bouncing off the river
Thud
Bounce,
Water bouncing off the hard, dirty mud.

It's raining!

Philip Smith (11)
The Robert Manning Technology College

Season!

S   is for the sizzling hot summer
E   is for the Easter eggs in spring
A   is for the angel on the Christmas tree
S   is for Christmas shopping
O   is for the orchestra at the concert
N   is for the autumn nut that fell off the tree.

Elizabeth Kirby (11)
The Robert Manning Technology College

FIRST DAY AT SCHOOL

The teachers all get ready
All those names to learn
They hope they're not too strict for them
Are the coat pegs clearly named?

The mums get the worries
They hope their kids are all right
Did they get lost?
They will be pleased to see their kids
Tonight.

The kids begin to cry
Who will be in my class?
I can't wait to see my mummy
I can't find my coat Miss.

Laura Turner (12)
The Robert Manning Technology College

RAINFOREST!

R oaming around on the ground below,
A nimals of all sizes, tall and low,
I watch them closely, but move very slowly,
N ot making a sound and stepping very lightly,
F orever getting lost in the gigantic leaves,
O nly scampering slowly upwards to the top of the canopy,
R aindrops fall onto my head, I see the arrival of the storm,
E mergents shelter me as I watch the night sky form,
S uddenly torrential rainstorms pass by,
T he night becomes clear and calm across the sky.

Vicki Bennett (14)
The Robert Manning Technology College

THE WIND

Whistling, whispering
as soft as silk.
Hustling, bustling,
through the trees.
Moaning. Groaning,
like he's been hurt.
Roaring. Howling,
against my door.
Screaming. Shouting,
down my chimney.
Whirling. Blowing,
against my window.
I can hear,
Thunder,
and lightning.
I feel afraid.

Emma Robinson (12)
The Robert Manning Technology College

A RAINY DAY

I glared out of the window,
The dew on the grass looked like a million diamonds sparkling away.
The grass was a lush green,
It almost looked good enough to eat.
But then it started to rain,
It was coming down like water from a tap.
It was drumming down on the window,
It looked as if it was trying to get in,
I walked away and slumped down on the couch,
I wanted to go out and play,
But it was raining.

Thomas Younghusband (11)
The Robert Manning Technology College

CATS

C is for cute and cuddly on a nice, hot day
A is for angry when you take their food away
T is for tame unlike tigers in the wild
S is for sweet - says any little child.

Cats are lovely and cuddly you know
They are nice to see playing in the snow.
Cats are pretty in all different colours but even better in black
But some people call them a witch's cat.
Black on the outside may look boring, plain and dull
But that's not what counts.
What counts is their personality on the inside.

Daniella Tuohy (11)
The Robert Manning Technology College

DEER

As I was wandering the woods,
I thought there was something near,
As I turn around,
In front of me was a deer,
This deer was a beautiful looking animal,
Coloured brown and grey,
I stepped a little closer,
It leaped up and ran away,
I chased the deer across the woods,
Trying to get near,
but the deer kept running away,
Because it was full with fear,
So I left it alone instead,
And he wandered off scared, to his bed.

Michaela Nichols (11)
The Robert Manning Technology College

OUR WORLD

Take a look at the world
Remember it is our home,
But how do we treat it
Not like a friend but an enemy.

We pollute the sea with sewage
And the sky with harmful gases.
When will we stop and realise
The damage and harm we cause.

Look after our world
Before it's too late
Stop the pollution
And harm we create.

If only we had listened
To the warnings of disaster
To our beautiful world
Our selfish needs did destroy!

Abigail Clarke (12)
The Robert Manning Technology College

POEM EXCUSES

The reason I'm late Sir is well,
First my grandad had a heart attack,
Then the dog tried to eat the cat.
And when I thought I was in luck,
An alien came and picked me up,
Well, Sir, I'm here anyway,
And no one really had to pay.
Also, Sir, my grandad had an operation,
So please, Sir, don't give me a detention.

Claire Green (12)
The Robert Manning Technology College

THE WOMBAT

He was walking through the Australian bush
when he received a little push.
When he turned around he was surprised
at what he found.

A little lizard as right as rain
making jokes that are very lame.
'What happens to a wombat that
crosses a road? . . . He gets squashed,' he said.

As I said he was very lame.
He also had a very strange name.
Lambert is what he was called
very strange and very small.

William Blair Green (11)
The Robert Manning Technology College

MY DOGS

My dogs Buster and Woody
Play with a bone that's Stringy,
They eat lots of milky bones
and sugary scones,
They like cuddles and
wrapping us up in muddles,
They have lots of toys
for furry boys
And plenty of things
we all *love!*

Natasha Williams (11)
The Robert Manning Technology College

THE RIVER FRESHNEY

T he wonderful river Freshney.
H ow fresh and clean it is.
E veryone likes the Freshney.

R ivers make people relax
I find the river so calming
V ery full of life
E verything that lives in it has found some peace at heart
R omantic river is so quiet.

F reshney can be so much fun
R ivers are the best
E ven to throw a stone
S toned and cobbled the base of it is
H ave some fun by the river
N ever ever fall in
E veryone loves the river
Y ouths and old folks alike.

Daniel Broughton (13)
Whitgift School

WRESTLING

W restlers rage in the ring,
R aw is war.
E xcitement mounting,
S lamming, shouting.
T ombstones, powerbombs and piledrivers
L ights flashing, bodies crashing.
I njured wrestlers carried away,
N ew champions made today,
G reat sport.

Wesley Aisthorpe (12)
Whitgift School

DIVISION

The world is divided
People are so undecided
So here's a poem about all the nations
Why do we need all these complications?

Why do we need the barrier of race?
Why don't we let all people go all over the place?
Colour and size does not matter
A person is the same whether thinner or fatter

Religions of the world all meet
Some rebel, not happy to meet
Catholics and Protestants throw hatred and more
Leaving other innocent ones injured and sore

So I suppose the message I'm trying to give in this poem
Is everyone should just keep on going
Whether we are a different religion, size or race
We should all get along, we live in the same place.

Jessica Cornford (13)
Whitgift School

WINTER

Winter is cold,
One big area becomes white with snow,
In the new year we go to our friends,
This year's turkey is huge for Christmas,
This happens every year,
For the weather rain, snow and fog are on the forecast.

Sam Engledow (12)
Whitgift School

ME VS YOU

Me versus you,
What shall we do?
Let's have a fight,
Here tonight.

Me versus you,
What shall we do?
Let's make friends
And hope the friendship never ends.

Me versus you,
What shall we do?
You go to Neptune,
And I'll go to the moon.

Me versus you,
What shall we do?
We are just like any opposites,
I suppose we sometimes have to mix.

Louise Kerrison (13)
Whitgift School

AUTUMN

Autumn comes and summer goes.
Under the trees there's lots of leaves.
The children all come out to play
Under the trees they play with the leaves.
Morning is back with a breath of fresh air
Now it's time to have more fun!

Madeleine Smith (12)
Whitgift School

HUMAN DIVISION

If you study the vast darkness of such a tiny place,
You begin to realise each life form has its own important place.
Too much time do we spend on criticism,
And not enough on exceptance.
As if we all condemn ourselves due to our race and religions,
The Earth that is ours to share
Shall be dismantled and left so bare?
If people can hurt others in anguish or hatred for their nation's
previous actions,
No one shall have compassion or grace to care,
Children are influenced by early distractions.
Do we want our future nations
To condemn us due to our present demonstrations?
Life is too precious to waste,
We each need to try and light this vast darkness we call hatred,
Jake back what was demonstrated,
And learn to care for each other,
For the Earth is our mother,
And she we need to respect.
Treat different as a gift,
And nurture it like talent.
If we stand shoulder by shoulder,
Surely our nation simply couldn't falter?

Kelly Bovill (13)
Whitgift School

FAMILY

Your family is always there for you
When things are looking tough
They buy you presents, take you out
But most of all give you their love.

Your family is always there for you
When times are good or bad
When you're around your family
Nothing ever seems sad.

Rebecca Everitt (11)
Whitgift School

A POEM ABOUT CLEETHORPES

C   ome to Cleethorpes it's lots of fun
L   azy day in the sun
E   veryone has such fun
E   normous beaches
T   o laugh and play
H   ave an ice cream
O   n the prom
R   ide a donkey by the sea
P   addle in the water up to your knees
E   njoy the sunshine and the breeze
S   o come to Cleethorpes it's the bee's knees.

Alan Smith (12)
Whitgift School

LIBRARY

L   ibrarians are working
I   nside the library
B   ooks people borrow
R   eading as they learn
A   lot of education
R   eally easy, really hard
Y   ears of learning are for sure.

Matthew Duffy (12)
Whitgift School

AMERICA'S DISASTER

A nybody who is unhappy, has every right to be,
M any people have suffered because of this,
E verybody is crying,
R unning out of the way of danger,
I f anything this is wrong,
C rime is always worrying,
A nything could happen next,
S uch a terrible crime has been committed.

D ead - is all people can say
I f people are alive, they've got to be strong!
S omething is always wrong with this world,
A nd all people can say is why? *Why?*
S adness is all over their faces,
T errible things are happening to these people,
E verybody is moping around,
R uined buildings are scattered everywhere.

Stacey Walker (12)
Whitgift School

FOOTBALL

Football here,
Football there,
Football everywhere.

Michael Owen with his pace,
Oh he is so ace,

Steven Gerard has the face,
He'll beat your wonderful pace,
With your pulse rate he'll win,
Because he's a goal scoring king!

Alun Parkin (11)
Whitgift School

AUTUMN

Leaves are turning crispy and brown,
They make a relaxing crackling sound.
They twist and turn round and round,
As they fall to the ground.

Summertime is over,
Wintertime is near.
But we're right in the middle,
Autumn time is here.

The weather is getting colder,
As the world is getting older.
We will have to wait another year,
Until the summertime is yet again here.

Summertime is over,
Wintertime is near.
But we're right in the middle
Autumn time is here.

Wintertime is gaining fast,
Summertime has definitely past.
Autumn time is here again
There's only a little sun every now and then.

Summertime is over
Wintertime is near
But we're right in the middle
Autumn time is here.

Liann Drinkell (12)
Whitgift School

WINNIE THE POOH

W innie the Pooh,
I   s loving and kind,
N ever, ever is he sad,
N ags his friends to come and play,
I   n Hundred Acre Wood,
E eyore is moody,

T igger is bouncing all around,
H aving fun,
E very day,

P iglet is small and cute,
O wl is intelligent,
O n and on they play,
H aving fun every day.

Carmen Jade Glenn-Limb (12)
Whitgift School

LOVE AT FIRST SIGHT

On a cold and frosty morning
All my troubles are dawning
From the night before
When I was stood at the door
Talking to a gorgeous guy
I know now I wanna die.

When he spoke to me
I went weak at the knees
It was love at first sight
If only for one night
For I know I will never see him again
Life will never be the same.

Melissa Wesley (13)
Whitgift School

DANGEROUS DRAGONS

D angerous dragon saw through the night.
R aging fire spits out from their mouths.
A ll in a pack of six and eight.
G oing from side to side up and down and round.
O n rooftops so high they can see so far away.
N ow the fun must stop cos it's time for them to go.

Daniel Holdsworth (11)
Whitgift School

NEW YORK

N ew York got bombed,
E veryone was terrified.
W e had three minutes silence,

Y oung people roaring and trapped.
O ur dads are going to war,
R aining pieces of rubble.
K illed and hurt people.

Peter Jones (12)
Whitgift School

ZODIAC

Z odiac is a sign in the stars,
O n a dark sky.
D ifferent patterns shining brightly,
I ndividual shapes and sizes.
A ries, Gemini, Taurus, Sagittarius,
C ancer, Capricorn, Leo and many more.

Michael Blakey (12)
Whitgift School

AMERICAN DISASTER

This is a poem for all the people who died
For all the people who stood and cried.
But when that plane circled and crashed
Everyone looked and their hearts slashed.
And the poor people who were sealed inside
The people down below started to run and hide.
All that was on the street was cloudy smoke
One man came out and started to choke.
All those families that are lost and gone
I wish they hadn't gone to work all along.
But nature went the wrong way
And now everyone has had a horrible and scary day.

Sophie Bilenkyj (12)
Whitgift School

AMERICA

September the 11th 2001,
Something in the world went very wrong.
At first the people were working away,
Doing their jobs they do every day,
And then it happened,
That terrible thing.
Death and destruction came within,
I know that this happened far away,
It will not be forgotten,
For each and every day
Because of all the people,
That died on that day.

Ashley Kiff (12)
Whitgift School

SPROUTS AND PEAS

Some people are fat, not thin.
Some people have dark skin.
Some people are as brave as a knight.
Some people get afraid at night.

If people hear thunder and lightning,
They find it very frightening.
Some people hug their cats,
Others hide under hats.

Most people want to end war,
Some people support the poor.
Some people like to sail the seas,
Some people prefer sprouts to peas!

Lauren Forsyth (13)
Whitgift School

WINTER DAYS

W inter is coming,
I   t's so near.
N ow's the time to wrap up warm,
T   oo cold for T-shirts,
E   veryone is freezing,
R   ain is all it ever does.

D ays are short,
A nd nights are long.
Y awning in the frosty morning,
S   chool is the worst thing of all.

Carley Barton (12)
Whitgift School

America 'Bombed'!

Tuesday 11th of September 2001
'Twin Towers would never be bombed' they said
Disaster had struck!
Everything depended on luck
The towers were burning
People were in shock and tummies were turning
Many crying
Because people were dying
Lots couldn't look
They were in the Twin Towers stuck
Waiting to die
As they heard the fire engine sigh
After an hour the towers had collapsed
The pain was 1000 times worse than being slapped
The smoke was as white as a clean sheet
Lots in heaven will meet
What has this world come to?
I can't believe this is what people do.

Sophie Stead (12)
Whitgift School

The Day

L   ots of things to do.
O   ver the hours.
N   o time to waste.
G   one into the night.

D   ay is all gone.
A   fter the dark the sun is here.
Y   ou are in the light.

Matthew Brusby (12)
Whitgift School

WINTERTIME

Winter, the time of coldness.
The time of icy days.
With the icicles shining and glittering
And the ice so thick.
Wintertime is here!

Winter the time of frosty days.
The time for snow and dew.
With the kids ducking and diving.
As the snowballs fly.
Kids go down in the war of snowballs
Wintertime is here.

Winter the time of Christmas.
The time of fun and joy
And Christmas presents under the tree.
Wintertime is here.

John Read (12)
Whitgift School

CHRISTMAS

C   hristmas is coming
H   ip, hip hooray
R   unning round the garden
I   n amongst the trees
S   anta is coming
T   omorrow it's Christmas Day
M   any of our relatives here to stay
A   ll of us are happy
S   o let's have a cracking day.

Zak Wilson (12)
Whitgift School

LIVING ON THE STREETS!

I'm hungry, I'm thirsty
I have no such luxury as a bed
My life is not worth living
I'm better off dead
I roam the streets in search of a meal
At night passers-by can hear me squeal
I long for scraps of chips, a loaf of bread
A nice, warm room to rest my head.

People snub me, look away.
Looks like I'm on the streets another day.
I don't want your pity, I don't want your worry
I'm just begging for your money.
Not for the drink, it's not for the booze
I promise I'll spend it on some food.

I can just dream and pray to the Lord
That one day my home won't be made of cardboard.
Until that day comes
I'll live in a slum
Until bricks and mortar will keep me warm.

Samantha Page (13)
Whitgift School

ACTING

A t the theatre there's a show
C an we see it Mum? Can we go?
T oday, tomorrow, the day after
I n the crowds cheers of laughter
N early over - curtain down
G oing home - the cast their bows.

Josh Morter (12)
Whitgift School

DIVISION

Black or white?
Why do we have race?
I think it's a disgrace,
How such people can judge,
By the colour of one's skin,
Or if they're fat or thin.

Catholic or Protestant?
They are the same? It's just a different belief,
If the arguments would stop and we could all be friends,
It would be a huge relief.

Rich or poor?
Why does it matter who's got more?
We all lead very different lives,
Some of us are well off,
And some are deprived.

This is a poem about the world in which we live,
The happiness in the world we should give,
We should all live together in harmony,
Whatever colour, size or race we happen to be.

Chelsee Thompson (13)
Whitgift School

CHRISTMAS

Christmas is near - everyone likes it.
Christmas is great - it is like your birthday.
Christmas is brilliant because of the cakes and chocolate.
Christmas cake is great but the Christmas dinner is better.
Christmas is the best because you get a lot of presents.
Christmas is brilliant because of the snow.

Matthew Taylor (12)
Whitgift School

AUTUMN

Golden leaves falling from beautiful trees
Trees become bare.
The golden and yellow leaves lying on the floor -
Nice and crunchy.
When you wake up in the morning it is,
Crispy and frosty.
Chilly mornings you can smell the breeze
Animals go into hibernation
Bronze conkers falling from the trees,
Hallowe'en comes - scary costumes.
Trick or treating - sends a shiver up my spine,
Parties, watching scary movies, balloons here and there.
Then comes my grandad's birthday
More parties come icing on the cake 'yum yum'!

Lauren Hallam (12)
Whitgift School

SNOW FUN

As people are asleep in their beds.
Snow fell and made a cold wet blanket.
As the sun rises robins sing a calm song.
A gentle breeze came through the village.
People awake in total silence.
Children run out of their homes,
Snowballs are made, snowmen too.
Then after a long day of fun the sun died
And the moon sprung out like a spring.
People go to bed as darkness comes
And wait for another day to come.

Jade Croft (12)
Whitgift School

CAN WE CHANGE?

If people would all join together,
Respect each one's beliefs and creed,
Give each person another chance
To help people in their time of need.

When conflicts occur and people fight
And rebels feel no shame
People hurt from this angry might
The fighters are to blame.

Brave are the people who speak out
And not use any violence
Maybe they can change the world
And break a racist silence.

Lucy Hawkins (13)
Whitgift School

DOES IT MATTER?

The world is a city full of streets
of people good and bad,
does it matter if you're black or white?
You should be glad of what you have.

Does it matter if you're rich or poor,
or if you're fat or thin
if you're old or if you're young
or if you lose or win?

Does it matter if you're thick or bright
or the world's at war
or if you're wrong or if you're right?
What does it matter for?

Lisa-Marie Hainesborough (13)
Whitgift School

CANDLES

Colourful rays dancing in the air,
Natural light flowing everywhere.
Candle light is such a sight,
That gets blown out at night.

Yeah, this is candlelight alright,
Watch the colours glow so bright.
Yellow, orange, red and white,
Purple, blue, smoke in fright.

Wet wax creeping down the side,
Forms a clump at the end of the ride.
When the candle is blown out,
The smell will linger all about.

Jenny Inkson (11)
Whitgift School

RAIN, RAIN

Rain, rain
down the drain
on my glass windowpane
don't drizzle, don't splash
give me sunshine at last!

Rain, rain
on the plain
smacking hard like a cane
don't drizzle, don't splash
give me sunshine at last!

Lauren Baker (11)
Whitgift School

The Morbid Soldier Song

Spending hours preparing kit
Darning a hole in a mit
Packing it up just in time
To get on the lorry that takes me to the front line
In the lorry I hear shells dropping all around
Penetrating and blowing up the ground
On and on onto my death
By bullet or chef
Whichever way I look at it
I'm gonna die.

Rory Lynch (13)
Whitgift School

Autumn

Autumn is very cool
Queues of leaves as they fall
All the trees are bare
Everywhere under trees you see leaves
All these muddy fields are covered with leaves
This happiness comes every year.

Lloyd Suddaby (12)
Whitgift School

Duane

D   uane is sometimes naughty.
U   sually he is quite good.
A   nd he never says no to football.
N   ever underestimates his mates.
E   normous chocolate fan.

Duane Stepan (13)
Whitgift School

SOME PEOPLE . . .

Some people are stronger than others,
Some people are black not white.
Some women long to be mothers,
Some people long for their sight.

Some people are fat, not thin,
Some people are rich, not poor.
Some people are scared of lightning,
And also the thunder's roar!

Some people go to heaven not hell,
Some people are bad not good.
At school they did very well,
Because they did what they should.

There is no difference between black and white,
Although narrow-minded people think so.
You may think they look a fright
But they're just the same as you, you know.

Rebecca Blakey (13)
Whitgift School

AUTUMN

Finally it's turned into *autumn!*
It's a cold, chilly, foggy night.
I can hear the early fireworks like
Rockets in the distance. I can hear the owl hooting.
The men from the pub screaming like wild animals.
The fresh wind brushes past me like a fan.
The trees start to die and the leaves frizzle and crunch.
They fall like a snowflake frozen in the wind.

Nathan Coulam (12)
Whitgift School

How The Other Half Live!

Rich is rich
Poor is poor
Unfortunate people
With houses with no door
Living on a crummy street
Ragged clothes to wear
And no shoes on their feet
Their lives full of despair
Hardly any edible food
Or any clean water to drink
Insects and filthy bugs, coming
Up through the sink.

Rich people are lucky
They have everything they need
From food to water to cleaning accessories
They even have a cute dog with a posh lead.

This is what life is like nowadays
Rich and poor divided
Why does everything in this stupid cruel world
Have to be double sided?

Kelly Crosby (13)
Whitgift School

Going Through The Winter

W   hite as snow.
I   cy like the icing on a cake.
N   ew Year's Eve.
T   reading snow into the house.
E   veryone is having a good time.
R   un away from snowballs.

Dion Sellars (12)
Whitgift School

PEACE

Peace shines around the world.
Peace lets the birds tweet in high trees - facing the wind,
Peace lets people live in harmony.
Peace lets people laugh around the world.
Peace lets dogs be walked in *peace!*

Richard Gilby (12)
Whitgift School

WINTER

W ind always appears and that's when I start my tears.
I go out to play and that's where I stay.
N ever see an animal running around the field.
T rees are so bare and leaves are so crunchy.
E veryone is playing with snow and that's when I glow.
R unning around the leaves as I hear 'crunch' below my knees.

Sian Steer (12)
Whitgift School

AUTUMN

A utumn winds blowing leaves across the ground
U nder trees, leaves lay like thousands of spilled paints
T he trees becoming bare, making room for new life
U ntouched the leaves continue their journey - carried by wind
M ore and more fly over the lake - few falling to the surface
N ow all is still and the leaves start to grow. Winter is here.

Michael Allenby (12)
Whitgift School

ROMEO AND JULIET

The two families were at war,
Romeo and Juliet didn't want any more,
They'd fallen in love,
Like two turtle doves,
Romeo fought and killed Tybalt,
Banished from Verona,
It wasn't his fault.

Juliet took sleeping potion,
In slow motion.
They thought she was dead,
That day she was supposed to be wed.

Romeo heard his true love had died,
So he bought some poison, and cried.
It was his last breath
Before death.

Juliet awoke to see him lying,
On his death bed.
She grabbed his dagger and
Stabbed herself until she bled.

Now their souls are together
In heaven we stay
Entwined forever
We hope, we pray.

Kym Elshaw (13)
Whitgift School

WHAT IF?

What if good was the same as bad
And you couldn't tell whether you were happy or sad,
What if heaven was the same as hell,
I guess we'll never be able to tell.

What if night was the same as day
And November was as sunny as May,
What if salad was as fattening as chips
And cars could sail like ships.

What if black was the same as white
And what if touch was the same as sight,
What if cats were the same as dogs
And what if flies weren't eaten by frogs.

What if everything was the same,
It wouldn't have its own name,
What if nothing was unique,
Would our minds remain bleak?

Samantha Jane Kerrison (13)
Whitgift School

FRIENDS FOREVER

A memory lasts forever, never does it die,
true friends stay together, never say goodbye,
a friend is someone you can trust, and tell your secrets to,
a friend is someone who stands by you
and doesn't leave you alone.

A true friend will help you in a sticky situation,
and when times are rough, they always help.
If you need a shoulder to cry on
they should be waiting with open arms and sympathy
and they'll be there for you as long as you need.

I need my friends, all through to the end
we'll be friends forever,
and the memories will never die,
I can trust my friend and tell secrets too,
my friend are always there,
and are always willing to help,
my friends are true, do you have any?

Laura Strandt (13)
Whitgift School